Using Reason's™ Virtual Instruments:
Skill Pack

Matt Piper

THOMSON
—————★—————™
COURSE TECHNOLOGY
Professional ■ Technical ■ Reference

Using Reason's™ Virtual Instruments:
Skill Pack

Publisher and General Manager, Thomson Course Technology PTR: Stacy L. Hiquet

Associate Director of Marketing: Sarah O'Donnell

Manager of Editorial Services: Heather Talbot

Marketing Manager: Mark Hughes

Senior Editor: Mark Garvey

Marketing Coordinator: Adena Flitt

Development Editor: Orren Merton

Project Editor and Copy Editor: Kim V. Benbow

Technical Reviewer: Vince Fierro

PTR Editorial Services Coordinator: Erin Johnson

Interior Layout: Shawn Morningstar

Cover Designer: Mike Tanamachi

CD-ROM Producer: Brandon Penticuff

Indexer: Kevin Broccoli

Proofreader: Marta Justak

ISBN-10: 1-59863-282-5
ISBN-13: 978-1-59863-282-8
Library of Congress Catalog Card Number: 2006927152
Printed in the United States of America
07 08 09 10 11 TW 10 9 8 7 6 5 4 3 2 1

THOMSON

COURSE TECHNOLOGY

Professional ■ Technical ■ Reference

Thomson Course Technology PTR, a division of Thomson Learning Inc. 25 Thomson Place Boston, MA 02210

http://www.courseptr.com

*This book is dedicated to my lifelong friend Steve Pacey,
who in 1991 showed me how to use an Atari computer
to program MIDI sequences.*

Acknowledgments

Thanks to everyone at Thomson Course Technology for giving me the opportunity to write this book, which has been quite a rewarding experience. In particular, it was a joy to work with Orren Merton, whose immensely helpful feedback and encouragement every step along the way ensured that I never felt like I was working on this project alone! Also thanks to Vince Fierro, whose careful technical reviewing helped me rest assured that my instructions made sense and actually worked, no matter how late at night I may have been writing them. Thanks to Kim Benbow for, once again, being a pleasure to work with. Thanks to Loui Westin of Propellerhead who was helpful above and beyond the call of duty with extremely detailed and knowledgeable answers to my questions. Thanks to Laura Escudé for turning me on to some of her favorite titles from her extensive technical library, which provided food for thought as I prepared to write this book. Many thanks to Calvin Banks who has been a part of so many of the most important opportunities that have come my way in the last couple of years. Thanks to World Ambient Symphony and Poobah Records for providing several chances to try out my homemade Reason sounds in public during the course of writing the book. Finally, very special thanks to Duncan Laurie, Steve Nalepa, Casey Kim, Evan "Bluetech," and Raul Resendiz (www.MySpace.com/3rdegreeProductions) for graciously providing additional loop content for the CD.

About the Author

Matt Piper has indulged his passion for music technology as a recording engineer, music producer, studio owner, musician/composer, and experimental music promoter since moving to Los Angeles in 1991. He joined the Thomson Course Technology family in 2005 with the publication of *Reason 3 Power!* which he co-authored with Michael Prager. Piper can currently be found in music venues around town using his laptop and other electronics to make strange psychedelic sounds with various improvisational groups.

Table of Contents

Located on the CD-ROM

Contents

Introduction

Reason is an amazing and unique electronic music production program that can be found in thousands of studios all over the world. With so many people using it, you may be considering how you will be able to put your own personality into your work with the program. What will distinguish the sounds you make in Reason from the rest of the crowd? The goal of this book is to give you the knowledge you need to freely express yourself with Reason, to get you out of the presets and into designing your own sounds. What may now appear to be a somewhat overwhelming jumble of virtual knobs, sliders, and buttons will soon become a finite and comfortable environment in which you can let your creativity soar. By the end of this book, you will know exactly what to do with every square inch of the Reason instruments. There will be no dark, murky corners of uncertainty. You will know what this or that knob does, and, when you adjust it and the sound changes, you will understand why it changed. Reason will be a tool that feels comfortable in your hands.

What Makes Reason Unique?

If you have experience using various DAWs (digital audio workstations), such as Pro Tools, Cubase, Logic, or SONAR, you are probably aware that there are dozens of virtual instruments and software-based samplers available for use with those programs. Examples of some virtual instruments would include Kontakt from Native Instruments, M-Tron from GForce, Atmosphere from Spectrasonics, iDrum from iZotope, Minimoog from Arturia, Halion from Steinberg—the list goes on and on. While many of these instruments are truly excellent in their sonic quality and creativity, you may have noticed something about using them. Once you load two or three or four of them into your DAW as plug-ins, your CPU performance meter starts to get pretty high; before you know it, you hear pops and clicks and stutters in your audio as your computer struggles to survive the pounding it is receiving. Also, each of these instruments has its own learning curve, and the connectivity and interaction between them is limited, in part, by whatever DAW you are using.

Reason is different. It is an all-you-can-eat synth bar! With a reasonably fast computer, you can put together just about as many synths, drum machines, sample players, and effects within Reason as you could ever want to. All these instruments and effects are loaded in the same "rack" and can be connected in countless different ways. The virtual instruments in Reason can control each other and be processed by each other in nearly any imaginative and experimental fashion of which you may conceive. And with Reason's Combinator, you can design your own synths in easy and intuitive ways, basically by putting together as many different existing synths as you want in any way you want, through whatever effects you desire, and saving the whole tower of power under one Combinator patch. So not only do you have all the powerful instruments included in Reason, but you can also quite easily build your own. Go crazy, folks! Engage in decadent synth gluttony. The learning curve is not too steep, and the possibilities are limitless.

About This Book

There are some things that this book assumes. It assumes that you have some basic working knowledge of Reason. It assumes (at least), that you can play the Reason demo song and hear sound come out of your speakers or headphones. It assumes you own a MIDI keyboard that can interface with your computer so that when you play some notes on the keyboard, you hear sound come out of Reason. It assumes that if you have any trouble with any of this basic operational stuff, you will look in the Reason Operation Manual for the answers.

There are some things that this book does not assume. It does not assume you have taken any classes on sound synthesis or electronics. It does not assume that you are fluent in techno-babble. It does not assume that you have used any music production software prior to purchasing Reason. The goal here is to provide a depth that will be truly satisfying to the seasoned pro, while delivered in a manner that is accessible and engaging to the layman.

The CD that accompanies this book contains sample content (audio files) for building your own NN-XT, NN-19, and Redrum patches. It also contains several finished patches for all the Reason instruments, as well as examples designed to allow you to check yourself as you progress through the various exercises and examples. By the way, the word "patch" (in this context) pretty much just means "preset" or "program." It is common to use the word patch because in the old days you actually had to "patch in" (plug in, unplug, re-plug) cables like an old-fashioned switchboard operator to make things happen with your old 100-lb analog synth setup. In addition to the example patches and song files, the CD contains appendices on NN-19 and Dr.Rex, both of which are actually complete chapters prepared with the same care (and format) as the other chapters in the book, including example files and sample content. There is also a brief appendix detailing how you can make your own ReFills out of the patches you create. Finally, the CD contains over 200 MB of additional sample content made by cutting-edge music producers, which you are free to use to create your own Reason songs.

Using Reason's Virtual Instruments: Skill Pack focuses intensely on the Reason instruments, hopefully with a depth, clarity, and usefulness that will distinguish it from other guides and make you glad you bought it. If you are looking for an overview of the entire Reason program, including sequencing, effects, mixing, and the like, you may find *Reason 3 Power!* (2005, Thomson Course Technology PTR) to be a useful companion to this book.

You may already have certain favorite Reason devices, or devices that you are especially interested to read about. Even though I respect these preferences, I would encourage you first to read Chapter 1, "The Subtractor." This chapter occurs first in the book for a purpose—it explains and demonstrates in great detail many of the most essential concepts you will need. You will recognize these concepts again and again as you explore the other Reason instruments, as well as synthesizers in general. Once you have thoroughly digested Chapter 1, the rest of the Reason instruments will be much easier to master.

The Subtractor

The first stop on our expedition deep into the heart of Reason's virtual instruments is the Subtractor (see Figure 1.1). From seriously super-deep bass sounds to warm, sweet, singing leads to sci-fi madness, this is a real meat-and-potatoes synth, modeled after classic analog synths of yesteryear. It's a great synth to sharpen your teeth on, and a favorite of mine. By the end of this chapter, you should have developed a comfortable hands-on feel for what synthesis is all about.

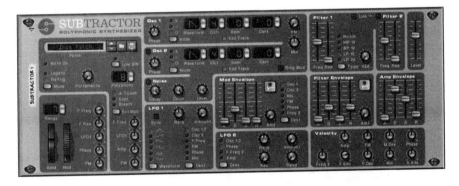

Figure 1.1
With a design inspired by classic analog synths, the Subtractor really delivers the goods.

Subtractor: What's in a Name?

The Subtractor uses what is known as *subtractive synthesis*. It's easy to remember this synth's name when you keep in mind that with subtractive synthesis, you start with a basic tone and then shape that tone by filtering out (or subtracting) various frequencies. There are three basic building blocks in subtractive synthesis:

- **Oscillator**—Generates the basic tone.
- **Filter**—Removes (or subtracts) frequencies from the basic tone generated by the oscillator.
- **Amplifier**—Amplifies the signal coming from the filter.

This may sound like science lab for another minute or two, but just hang in there. This is going to get very hands-on, like finger painting with sound. But it won't be any fun if we don't define our terms first and understand just what it is we are playing with. So before we get into sculpting our sound, let's take a look at the starting point or source of that basic sound: the Oscillator section.

Oscillator Section

The *American Heritage Dictionary* says that to oscillate is to "swing back and forth with a steady, uninterrupted rhythm." If you were to swing back and forth 20 times per second (at 20 Hertz, abbreviated Hz), the air you would be moving (the sound waves you would be creating) would be just at the bottom range of human hearing, considered a sub-bass frequency. If you moved back and forth (vibrated or oscillated) 440 times per second (440 Hz), you would achieve a low-mid frequency, and people could tune the A string of their guitars to you. You would probably be dead if you swung back and forth that fast to any great degree, but at least you would have died with perfect pitch, if that is any consolation.

An electronic oscillator does more or less the same thing, but with electricity. *American Heritage Dictionary*, to the rescue again, defines an oscillating circuit as "an electric circuit with values of capacitance and inductance that cause its current, charge, and electric potential to oscillate in a sinusoidal pattern." Sinusoidal? Is that like suicidal due to chronic sinus congestion? No, but good guess. If it occurred to you that "sinusoidal" reminds you of "sine wave," then you are on the right track. The Subtractor, of course, is using a mathematical emulation of an oscillating circuit to generate its tone, but it's the same general idea. Let's look at the Subtractor's Oscillator section (see Figure 1.2).

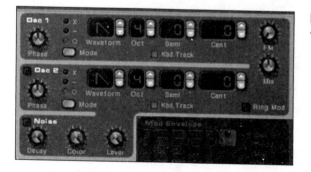

Figure 1.2

The Oscillator section of the Subtractor.

Oscillator 1

We will start by checking out Oscillator 1 hands-on. Start with an empty rack. I have the Default Song preference on the General Page of my Reason Preferences set for Empty Rack. You may wish to do the same.

1. Create an instance of the reMix mixer by choosing Mixer 14:2 from the Create menu. Since the Subtractor is mono (it has only one audio output instead of a stereo left/right output pair), it is nice to have the mixer there. This way you will not be stuck with the Subtractor only coming out of the left or right channel. reMix will have it panned in the middle of the stereo image by default.

2. Create an instance of Subtractor. In the Subtractor's Patch Browser window, you will see that it says Init Patch. This is the default patch. If, while working with Subtractor, you ever want to return to this starting point, you can right-click on the edge of the Subtractor (Ctrl-click on the Mac) and select Initialize Patch.

3. Turn the Freq slider of Filter 1 all the way to the top. This will effectively deactivate Filter 1. More later on why this is the case. For now, I just want you to be able to hear the various waveforms the Subtractor's oscillators can generate without any subsequent processing. Play a few notes on your MIDI keyboard or click on the piano keys in the Edit mode of the Sequencer to make sure you are getting some sound out of the Subtractor, and you are ready to continue (see Figure 1.3).

Figure 1.3

Just add a mixer and a Subtractor, and you are ready to try out some waveforms.

3

In the Init Patch, Oscillator 2 is not active. This is indicated by the fact that the little red light to the left of Osc 2 is dark. So we will only be hearing Oscillator 1 for the moment. Let's look at the controls on Osc 1.

Waveform Selector

Each of the two Subtractor oscillators gives you 32 waveforms to choose from. The currently selected waveform is displayed in the little window to the left of the selector up/down arrows. The first four of these waveforms (Sawtooth, Square, Triangle, and Sine) are standard waveforms that can be found on most analog synthesizers. Their actual shapes are displayed in the Waveform window. The other 27 waveforms were custom designed by Propellerhead. They are simply numbered 5 through 32. For Propellerhead's description of what they were aiming for with each of these waveforms, please consult your Reason Operation Manual, found in Reason Folder > Documentation > English. You could also just use your ears and imagination to listen to each of these waveforms and decide for yourself what you think they sound like and how they might be useful to you. I will take a moment to briefly discuss the first four "standard issue" waveforms:

Sawtooth—This waveform has all the harmonics (or overtones), making it the most complete of all waveforms. Its brightness really cuts through, and it is almost too hot to handle without some filtering.

Square—This waveform is mellower than the Sawtooth and contains the odd-numbered harmonics.

Triangle—This waveform is even mellower than the Square wave because it contains even fewer harmonics. Like the Square wave, the harmonics (or overtones) it does have are of the odd-numbered variety.

Sine—Oh Sine wave, how you rock my subwoofers with your smooth essential sound. The Sine wave contains no harmonics whatsoever, making it the simplest of all waveforms. In the mid-to-upper register, it is super smooth and mellow. Down low, you can really shake the house if you've got a good subwoofer. The Sine wave is as deep as it gets. And the Subtractor has a nice one!

You should already be set up to scroll though these waveforms by clicking on their respective up and down arrow buttons, then playing your MIDI keyboard a bit on each one to hear what it sounds like. Keep in mind that some of these waveforms may sound weird or harsh right now, but you have not yet begun filtering them, shaping them, or mixing them.

Keyboard Tracking and Tuning Controls

Near the center bottom portion of Oscillator 1 is the Keyboard Tracking button labeled Kbd.Track. If you deactivate this, then the oscillator will not react to note pitch information, but only to note on/off information. Thus every key you hit will produce the same note. Leave Keyboard Tracking on if you still want to be able to play a major scale. You may, however, program some percussive sounds or special effects patches for which turning off Keyboard Tracking may be appropriate.

In addition to the Keyboard Tracking button, the following three controls also affect oscillator pitch:

- **Octave**—Raises or lowers the pitch of the oscillator by 12 semitones per step.
- **Semi**—Raises or lowers (transposes) the pitch of the oscillator by one semi-tone (or note) per step.
- **Cent**—Think of this as fine-tuning. If both oscillators are active, you can create chorusing effects by pitching one oscillator a few cents differently than the other. A cent is 1/100th of a semitone.

HARMONICS AND OVERTONES

In the preceding description of the Subtractor's waveforms, I made reference to harmonics and over-tones. Harmonics are multiples of the original (or *fundamental*) tone. A pure sine wave contains only the fundamental tone, also known as the *first harmonic*. The second harmonic of a 440 Hz sine wave would be 880 Hz. A harmonic is a type of *overtone*, but an overtone is not always a harmonic. That is, an overtone may not always be an exact integer multiple of the fundamental tone. It could instead be a *partial* (or *inharmonic*) overtone. In either case, overtones (harmonic and inharmonic) determine the timbre, or tonal, characteristics of the sound. Each stop you pull out on an organ adds more harmonics to the sound. Opening up a *low pass filter* (raising the *cutoff frequency*) also allows more harmonics to become audible. You have probably also heard guitarists play harmonics, either while tuning or during performance.

Phase Offset Modulation

Please notice the two Phase knobs. There is one for Osc 1, and another for Osc 2. If you know anything about phase relationships (perhaps in the context of speaker placement or microphone placement), then you might suspect that these phase knobs control the phase relationship between Oscillator 1 and Oscillator 2. This is not actually the case. The real deal is that in addition to generating a single waveform, each of the Subtractor oscillators is capable of generating a second waveform (within the same oscillator) identical to the one selected in the Waveform window. When we talk about *phase*, we are referring to the point in time at which the waveform begins a new cycle. So when we talk about the *phase relationship* between two waveforms, we are talking about what point in time one waveform begins a new cycle in relation to the point in time the second waveform begins a new cycle.

Imagine a visual representation of a sine wave painted on an animation cell (a clear sheet of plastic). Now imagine a second sine wave painted on a second animation cell placed on top of the first. In this scenario, when the Phase knob is set at zero, the second sine wave is located directly over the top of the first, perfectly aligned, so it appears as if you can only see one sine wave (shown in Figure 1.4). When you begin to move the Phase knob to the right, you move one of those animation cells to the right. So now you can see both waveforms, and you can see the offset (the phase offset) between them (shown in Figure 1.5).

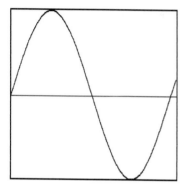

Figure 1.4
Two identical sine waves with no phase offset.

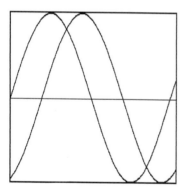

Figure 1.5
Two identical sine waves with their phases offset.

We are not only offsetting the phase of the two waveforms with the Phase knob (or Phase Offset Amount knob), but we are also either subtracting one offset wave from the other or multiplying one wave by the other, thus creating an entirely new waveform. The method used for creating this new waveform will be determined by the Mode button. By default, the Mode button is in the O position, which means no phase offset modulation will occur. Here are the three selections that you can make with the Mode button:

- ■ **X Waveform Multiplication**—One waveform is multiplied by the other to create a new waveform.

- ■ **— Waveform Subtraction**—One waveform is subtracted from the other to create a new waveform.

- ■ **O No Waveform Multiplication or Subtraction**—The Phase knob has no effect whatsoever.

This X — O thing is not complicated, but you should try to get it straight now, or you may not understand it until much, much later.

Just think of math symbols: X multiplies, — subtracts, and O does nothing (no second waveform is produced, and the Phase knob has no effect).

Please note that if the mode is set for subtraction and if you do not turn up the Phase knob at all, one identically placed waveform will be subtracted from the other, leaving zero, which means no sound. In fact, let's hear that. Doing it may shed more light than talking about it at this point.

1. Start with an empty rack and then add reMix and Subtractor.

2. Subtractor should already have Init Patch loaded. Please turn Filter 1's Freq slider all the way up to the top (so that the Low Pass filter doesn't actually filter anything).

3. Oscillator 1 is active by default and set for a Sawtooth waveform. Turn Oscillator 1's Phase knob down to zero (all the way to the left). This has no effect so far because the Mode selector is set by default for 0 (no phase offset modulation).

4. Click the Mode button twice so that Waveform Subtraction (—) is selected. Hit a key on your MIDI keyboard, and you should hear nothing. Keep holding down a key or two; then slowly turn the Phase knob to the right with your mouse. You will hear the sound fade in and change as you go (see Figure 1.6).

5. Try the same thing again, but this time use the Mode button to select Waveform Multiplication (X), and listen to how the sound changes as you move the Phase knob back and forth. Experiment with using different waveforms while sweeping the Phase knob, both in Waveform Multiplication (X) mode and in Waveform Subtraction (—) mode.

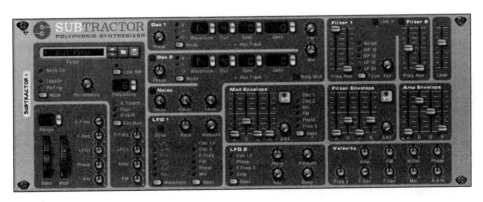

Figure 1.6

Waveform Subtraction is being applied to the two "offset wave-forms being produced by Oscillator 1.

You will notice that different waveforms react quite differently to phase offset modulation. You've barely covered a few square inches of the Subtractor, and already you are making some pretty crazy sounds!

WHERE'S THE MODULATION?

You may be asking the following very good question at this point: "I see that there is phase offset going on, and also waveform subtraction and multiplication, but where does the *modulation* come in?" If you were wondering about this, you get a gold star. (I hope they included some gold stars with this book.) The answer is, *You* are providing the modulation by sweeping the Phase Offset Amount knob back and forth. To *modulate* (most simply in this context) means to change or vary a characteristic. You are varying the amount of phase offset by dragging the Phase knob back and forth with your mouse, and that cool effect you hear is the result of that phase offset modulation. As this chapter progresses, you will learn several ways to apply various types of modulation, and most of them do not even require the use of your mouse!

Oscillator 2

We cannot get much farther in the Oscillator section without mentioning Osc 2. It has the same controls as Oscillator 1: Phase knob, Mode selector for phase offset modulation, Waveform selector, Octave, Semi, and Cent pitch controls, and a Keyboard Tracking button. In addition to these controls, it also has a Ring Mod button (more on this in the "Ring Modulation" section of this chapter), as well as its own on/off button (the red one to the left of where it says Osc 2). Also note that the FM Amount knob works in conjunction with the Osc 2 output.

The level of Oscillator 2's output is controlled by the Mix knob. The Mix knob does just what you might suppose it does. It mixes the signals between Osc 1 and Osc 2. If you turn it all the way to the left, you will only hear Osc 1. If you turn it all the way to the right, you will only hear Osc 2. In the middle, you will hear an even mix of the two oscillators (see Figure 1.7).

Figure 1.7
Subtractor's second oscillator adds more than double the fun.

Noise Generator

It is good to mention the Noise Generator right after talking about the Mix knob, because the output of the Noise Generator is routed through Osc 2. Even if Osc 2 is not activated, you can still hear the Noise Generator if it is turned on. So, just like Osc 2, any output from the Noise Generator will be loudest when the Mix knob is turned all the way to the right and will disappear when the Mix knob is turned all the way to the left.

The Noise Generator does not react to pitch information, so it sounds the same, no matter what key you press. It is also not controlled by the Amp Envelope (more on the Amp Envelope later). Instead, it has its own Decay knob, which determines how long the Noise Generator's sound will last when a note is played. The Noise Generator can be used to add "breath" to a flute patch, or it can be used for the attack of a percussion patch. It can also be included as wind noise in a pad or used in effects patches. In addition to its red on/off button, the Noise Generator has three controls:

- **Decay**—This determines how long the noise will last once a note has been played. Long decays can be used for wind noise, and short decays can be used when you want the Noise Generator to provide a percussive attack.

- **Color**—Think of this like a tone control (a simple EQ). Turning the knob to the left makes the sound darker (more bass). Turning it to the right makes the noise brighter (more treble).

- **Level**—This is the volume control for the Noise Generator. Once this knob is turned up (at least partway) you can additionally control the noise level with the Mix knob in the Oscillator section.

Frequency Modulation

In electronics, to *modulate* means to vary a characteristic (such as frequency, phase, or amplitude) of a signal. Implied in this term is that the modulated signal is being modulated by another signal. When you use the Frequency Modulation (FM) feature of the Subtractor, the frequency of Oscillator 1 is modulated by the frequency of Oscillator 2. Note that this effect occurs even if the Mix knob is turned all the way to the left (so that only Oscillator 1 can be heard). In fact, I think that's the most fun way to play with this one. The FM effect sounds so cool, so extreme, and has so many possibilities, I cannot refrain from jumping in and playing with it right now.

1. Start with an empty rack, and then add reMix and Subtractor.

2. Subtractor should already have Init Patch loaded. Please turn Filter 1's Freq slider all the way up to the top (so that the Low Pass filter doesn't actually filter anything).

3. Oscillator 1 is active by default and set for a Sawtooth waveform, which is fine by me. Click the little square button to the left of Osc 2 (it will light up red) to activate Osc 2, which is also set to a Sawtooth wave.

4. Turn the Mix knob all the way to the left so that only Osc 1 can be heard.

5. Hold down a note on your keyboard and ease the FM knob up and down to hear how the sound changes.

6. Now change the value of Osc 2's Semi parameter to 1 (one half step up). Again, ease the FM knob up and down to hear how the sound changes. It's starting to sound kind of sick, don't you think? It sounds extra cool if you sweep very slowly between FM values of zero and 60, especially as you transition from zero on up. Also notice that the sound (and rate of the "pulsing") changes, depending on what notes you play.

7. Change the value of Osc 2 Semi to 4. Experiment as you have before. Also try it with an Osc 2 Semi value of 5 (see Figure 1.8).

Figure 1.8

FM: It's not just for your radio anymore!

Before moving on, I would encourage you to experiment with different Osc 2 Semi settings, and I would also encourage you to try different combinations of Waveforms between Osc 1 and Osc 2 because they all interact differently.

Oscillator 2 is not the only signal source with which you can modulate the frequency of Oscillator 1. Since the Noise Generator's output is routed through Oscillator 2 (even when Oscillator 2 is deactivated), you can use the Noise Generator to modulate the frequency of Oscillator 1. Simply turn on the Noise Generator, turn up its level control, and turn up the FM knob. This will immediately shred your sound into ribbons of inharmonic mayhem. Maybe not so good for a pop love song, but it might turn out to be just the kind of chaos you were looking for.

Ring Modulation

Ring modulation is a type of amplitude modulation (AM). I always thought it got its name from the bell-like overtones it can produce, but it turns out that one way to build a ring modulator circuit involves arranging some of the electronic components in a ring, and that's where the name comes from. Ring modulation sounds rather technical, but it's actually pretty simple and can make some delightfully weird sounds. Here's how it works. Two signals are needed: a carrier signal (which is not heard) and an input signal (which may or may not be heard, depending on whether or not you decide to mix it in). Assuming you do not monitor the input signal, the actual Ring Modulator output signal is made up of two tones. One output tone's frequency is the sum of the carrier signal's frequency added to the input signal's frequency, and the second output tone's frequency is the difference between the carrier signal's frequency and the input signal's frequency. So if the input signal's frequency is 400 Hz and the carrier signal's frequency is 300 Hz, the Ring Modulator's output signal will be a complex waveform containing two pitches, 700 Hz (the sum) and 100 Hz (the difference). Don't feel bad if you have to read this paragraph a couple of times before you "get it." Pretty neat, though, don't you think? Let's hear it in action.

1. Start with an empty rack and then add reMix and Subtractor.

2. Subtractor should already have Init Patch loaded. Please turn Filter 1's Freq slider all the way up to the top (so that the Low Pass filter doesn't actually filter anything).

3. Turn on Osc 2 by clicking on its little red power button.

4. Set the waveform of Osc 1 to a Sine wave. The graphic in the Osc 1 Waveform selector should look like an "S" on its side.

5. Set the waveform of Osc 2 to a Triangle wave. The graphic in the Osc 2 Waveform selector should look like a mountain peak.

6. Turn the Mix knob all the way to the right so that Osc 1 (your input or modulation signal) cannot be heard. The frequency of Osc 2 (the carrier signal) will be modulated by the frequency of Osc 1.

7. Turn OFF the Kbd.Track button on Osc 2. This way the (unheard) carrier signal will be the same frequency, no matter what note you play on your keyboard.

8. Click the Ring Mod power button so it lights up red.

9. Set the octave of Osc 1 to a value of 6.

10. Play around on your MIDI keyboard. As you play, experiment with different values for the Semi parameter on Osc 1 (see Figure 1.9). Are you "blinded with science" yet?

Figure 1.9

Your Subtractor should look something like this at the end of the Ring Modulation exercise.

In case you want to check your work on the above exercise, I have saved a version (with an Osc 1 Semi setting of 11) under the patch name RingModScience in the Subtractor Patches folder on the included CD-ROM. To load the patch, simply open the Subtractor's Patch Browser by clicking on the little folder icon to the right of the Subtractor's Patch Display window. Then you can browse to the location where RingModScience.zyp is stored.

As with Frequency Modulation, you will find that Ring Modulation can produce a variety of effects, depending on which combination of waveforms and pitches you use. Speaking of Frequency Modulation, slowly bringing in a little bit of FM sounds delightfully weird when added to the exercise we've just been working on. Please take time to experiment while you are here. I will go make some coffee, and when you are done experimenting, we can explore the Filter section together.

Filter Section

Just like a coffee filter or a camera lens filter, an audio filter lets some things pass through and stops the rest. Your home stereo almost certainly has at least a couple of audio filters on it with which you are familiar. They are the Bass and Treble controls. When you turn down the bass on your stereo, you are using a *high pass filter*. The high frequencies pass through unaffected, but the low frequencies are filtered out according to how much you turn down the Bass knob. If you turn down the Treble control, you are using a *low pass filter*. Low frequencies pass through unaffected, but high frequencies are filtered out (or attenuated), depending on how much you turn down the Treble control. If you have used a PA system or professional mixing board, you may have noticed that on each microphone channel, there is a button that says something like Low Cut or 75Hz HPF. That is a high pass filter that lets frequencies above 75 Hertz (or thereabouts) pass unaffected, but it attenuates frequencies below 75 Hz, perhaps by a degree of 12 decibels or more per octave. This minimizes thudding "p" pops and low frequency rumble and feedback, while avoiding a "muddy" or unclear sound, especially for vocals (sung or spoken). Since the human voice doesn't generally go down that low anyway (James Earl Jones notwithstanding), these frequencies can be removed without substantially degrading the fidelity of the vocal performance.

In the world of sound synthesis, filters are used less for troubleshooting and more for artistic expression. These filters are not necessarily static. They are often adjusted in real time to dramatic effect. The Subtractor has two filters, which can be used independently of each other or in tandem.

As always, let's be ready to play with this stuff hands-on as we go. If you've already got reMix and Subtractor in your rack, then please initialize the Subtractor. To do this, right-click on the Subtractor (or Ctrl-click for Mac) and choose Initialize Patch. Alternatively, you can select Initialize Patch from the Edit menu. Then, in the Velocity section, turn down F.Env to zero (12 o'clock). You will see the little red light above it turn off. Now we are ready to take a detailed look at the filter action the Subtractor has to offer (see Figure 1.10).

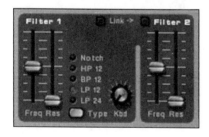

Figure 1.10

The Filter section of the Subtractor.

Filter 1

Filter 1 is the more flexible of the Subtractor's two filters. It has five filter types from which to choose, while Filter 2 is fixed as a single type (a 12 decibel Low Pass filter). Unlike Filter 2, Filter 1 also includes a Filter Keyboard Tracking function, allowing the Filter Frequency value to be affected by how high or low within the keyboard register you play. Filter 1 has the following controls:

- **Freq**—The Filter Frequency slider (also known as the *cutoff filter*) specifies where in the audio frequency spectrum the filter's effect will be focused. It determines the *cutoff frequency*. The cutoff frequency (in the case of a High Pass or Low Pass filter) is simply the frequency at which the filter begins to take effect. So in a High Pass filter, for example, the cutoff frequency will be the frequency at which the filter begins cutting off (or filtering out) low frequencies, while allowing high frequencies to pass through. In the case of a Notch or Band Pass filter, the term *cutoff frequency* is a bit confusing because the value of the Filter Frequency slider will really be determining the frequency at which the filter has the greatest effect, even though the filter will still be affecting a range of frequencies immediately above *and* below the cutoff frequency. The width of this range (the *bandwidth*) will be determined by the value of the Resonance slider (in the case of a Notch or Band Pass filter). This paragraph will make more sense if you reread it after you have read the following description of the five filter types.

- **Type**—The Filter Type button selects from among the following five filters:

  - **Notch**—The Notch filter rejects mid-frequencies (determined by the Freq slider) and allows frequencies above and below that "notch" to pass through. Use the Filter Type button to select the Notch filter. Hold down a chord on your MIDI keyboard and sweep the Filter Freq slider up and down to hear the effect. While the specific frequency at which the Notch filter's effect is concentrated is determined by the Filter Frequency slider, the size (or *bandwidth*) of the Notch is determined by the value of the Resonance slider.

  - **HP 12**—The 12-Decibel High Pass filter allows high frequencies to pass through, but attenuates (by 12 decibels per octave) frequencies below the frequency determined by the Filter Frequency (or cutoff filter) slider. The term *cutoff filter* makes more sense in this context. Use the Type button to select HP 12 and turn the Freq slider all the way down. You will hear no effect yet because the High Pass filter only filters frequencies *below* the cutoff frequency, and there is nothing below "all the way down"! Now hold down a chord on your MIDI keyboard and slowly turn up the Filter Frequency slider to hear the effect of the High Pass filter.

  - **BP 12**—The Band Pass filter is the opposite of the Notch filter. While the Notch filter selects a band (or group of frequencies) to filter out while allowing all other frequencies to pass through, the Band Pass filter selects a band (or group of frequencies) to pass through, while filtering out (attenuating by 12 dB per octave) frequencies above and below that band. As with the Notch filter, the specific frequency at which the Band Pass filter's effect is concentrated is determined by the value of the Filter Frequency slider, while the size of the frequency band (or *bandwidth*) is determined by the value of the Resonance slider. Please select BP 12, hold down a chord on your MIDI keyboard, and slowly move the Freq slider up and down to hear the effect of the Band Pass filter.

- **LP 12**—The 12-Decibel Low Pass filter allows low frequencies to pass through, but filters out high frequencies with a roll-off curve of 12 decibels per octave. This is a very nice filter to sweep, especially with a bit of resonance.

- **LP 24**— The 24-Decibel Low Pass filter allows low frequencies to pass through, but filters out high frequencies with a more extreme roll-off curve of 24 decibels per octave. This is also a very nice filter to sweep, especially with a bit of resonance. You can end up with some pretty big bass using this filter.

See, all these names make sense. Low Pass allows low frequencies to pass, High Pass allows high frequencies to pass, Notch "notches" out a specific band while allowing everything else to pass, and Band Pass allows a specified band to pass while filtering out all other frequency content. Now let's look at the rest of Filter 1.

- ■ **Res**—The Resonance slider is used to emphasize the frequencies specified by the Filter Frequency slider when using High Pass and Low Pass filters. To hear this effect, you can go through these filter types again, sweeping the Filter Frequency like you did before, but this time with the Resonance slider turned up. The Low Pass filters sound especially cool this way. Please be careful with your volume setting. You may make some surprisingly loud (and potentially painful or damaging) sounds this way. If there is a dog in the room, he should be wearing ear protection. If you noticed that the Resonance effect is not so strong with the Band Pass and Notch filters, this is because the Resonance slider affects these filters differently. Instead of emphasizing frequencies around the cutoff frequency, in the case of the Band Pass and Notch Filters, the Resonance slider determines the bandwidth. High Resonance settings will result in a narrower bandwidth (fewer frequencies above and below the cutoff frequency are affected), and low Resonance settings will result in a wider bandwidth (more frequencies above and below the cutoff frequency are affected).

- ■ **Kbd**—The Filter Keyboard Track knob determines to what extent (if any) the Filter Frequency is affected by which notes are played on your MIDI keyboard. When the Filter Keyboard Track knob is turned up, playing higher notes will result in slightly higher Filter Frequency settings, while playing lower notes will result in slightly lower Filter Frequency settings. The Filter Frequency slider will not move, but you will be able to hear the effect (that is, notes played higher on the keyboard sound brighter, while notes played lower on the keyboard sound darker or warmer).

- ■ **Link**—The Filter 2 Link button causes Filter 1 and Filter 2 to work together in the following manner. When the Link button is engaged, adjusting the Frequency slider of Filter 1 also adjusts the Frequency slider of Filter 2, while preserving the offset between the two filter's cutoff frequencies. By preserving the offset, I mean that if the Freq slider of Filter 1 starts at a value of zero, and the Freq slider of Filter 2 is set at a value of 20, whatever value you set Filter 1's Freq slider at, the cutoff frequency of Filter 2 will be 20 steps higher. However, you will never actually see Filter 2's Freq slider moving during all of this, but you can hear it with your ears. We will try an example of this in just a moment. First, let's take a look at Filter 2.

Filter 2

Filter 2 is a 12-decibel (dB) Low Pass filter. Unlike Filter 1, Filter 2 has no Filter Keyboard Track function. It does have an on/off button, and its Filter Frequency and Resonance sliders function the same as those of Filter 1. As previously stated, when the Filter 2 Link button is activated, Filter 2 Frequency is affected by the setting of Filter 1 Frequency.

Let's try out that Filter 2 Link button.

1. Start with an empty rack; then add reMix and Subtractor.

2. Subtractor should already have Init Patch loaded. In the Velocity section, turn down F.Env to zero (12 o'clock). You will see the little red light above it turn off.

3. Play a few keys on your MIDI keyboard. Now turn on Filter 2 by clicking the Filter 2 on/off button. Turn the Filter 2 Frequency slider all the way down. Play a few keys, and you will hear nothing because Filter 2 is filtering out everything above its cutoff frequency. Since the cutoff frequency is at its minimum, everything is filtered out.

4. Click on the Filter 2 Link button. Play a few keys, and you can hear again because the Filter 1 Frequency slider is also affecting the frequency of Filter 2.

5. Set Filter 1 Frequency to 49, Filter 1 Resonance to 73, Filter 1 Type to BP 12, and Filter 2 Resonance to 65.

6. Now play a rhythm on some low keys while you sweep Filter 1 Frequency between about 49 and 100 (see Figure 1.11).

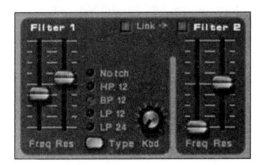

Figure 1.11

The Filter 2 Link button allows Filter 1 and Filter 2 to work together.

For your reference, an example of the above exercise "in action" is included on your CD-ROM. It is in the Subtractor In Action folder with the name Filter2LinkExample.rsn, which is a Reason Song File.

Envelope Section

When discussing sound and sound synthesis, the word *envelope* is used to describe the shape of a sound over time. The Subtractor has three envelopes to play with: the Amp Envelope, the Filter Envelope, and the Modulation Envelope (see Figure 1.12). You may be wondering what I mean by an envelope describing the *shape* of a sound over time. Imagine striking a large bell with a hammer. Think of the sound of this event happening in real time. At the beginning of the event is the initial strike. In envelope-speak, this is referred to as the *attack*. After the attack, the sound begins to fade out, or *decay*. This vocabulary, as you will read below, has been expanded to incorporate more detailed concepts, but you are probably starting to get a feel for where this is headed.

When we want to affect the volume (or amplitude) structure of the sound event over time, we will adjust the Amp Envelope. You may have been thinking in terms of volume or presence of sound as you considered the bell example. When we want to affect the tonal or frequency characteristics of a sound over time, we will be adjusting the Filter Envelope. And, of course, if we want to affect the manner in which modulation is applied to the signal over time, we will use the Modulation Envelope.

Figure 1.12

The Envelope Section of the Subtractor.

ADSR: Four Letters You Cannot Live Without

ADSR—these four letters stand for Attack, Decay, Sustain, and Release. Please say the words to yourself a few times if this concept is new to you. From here on out, you will see these four parameters again and again throughout Reason, and also on just about any analog or emulated analog synthesizer you ever use in the future. With these four parameters, you will sculpt quite a bit of your sound. If you take away nothing else from this book, I hope at least that this section will be clear in your mind for eternity. If you tell someone that you read this book, and that person asks you to show him how ADSR works in Reason, and you are unable to do so, then we will have both brought shame upon me, my ancestors, and all my future generations. No pressure, but with that in mind, please read on.

Amp Envelope

Perhaps the most familiar area in which to play with ADSR is the Amp Envelope (see Figure 1.13). An amplifier, in audio synthesis, makes a signal louder by increasing the amplitude of the signal. If you are looking at a sine wave on an oscilloscope, the amplitude will be the distance between the highest point and lowest point of one cycle of the sine wave. A shorter distance means a quieter signal, while a greater distance (a "taller") sine wave will result in a louder signal.

Figure 1.13
Attack, Sustain, Decay, and Release sliders shape the Subtractor's Amp Envelope.

While the Subtractor's Level control affects the overall volume (or amplification) of your sound, the Amp Envelope controls the shape of how that amplification is applied over time. Will the sound start sharply when you strike a key, or will it fade in slowly? Will it end abruptly when you let go of the key, or fade out slowly? Is a short sound produced, like a drum hit, or is a long, sustained tone produced, like holding down a key on an organ?

Here is how ADSR relates to the Amp Envelope. You can refer to this when considering other ADSR envelopes as well.

- **Attack**—The amount of time it takes for the amplitude of a sound to climb from zero to its peak level.

- **Decay**—The amount of time it takes for the amplitude of a sound to fall from its peak level to the level determined by the Sustain parameter, assuming you keep holding down the key(s).

- **Sustain**—At the end of a note's decay, the Sustain value determines the level at which the amplitude rests as long as the note is being held.

- **Release**—The amount of time it takes for the level of a sound to drop to zero from whatever level it was when you let go of a note.

The following exercise should make this all quite clear.

1. Start with an empty rack. Create an instance of the reMix mixer by choosing Mixer 14:2 from the Create menu, and then create an instance of Subtractor. In the Subtractor's Patch Browser window, it should say Init Patch.

2. Turn the Freq (frequency) slider on Filter 1 all the way up. In doing this, you are actually deactivating Filter 1. Why? Because the Filter Type control on Filter 1 is set for LP 12, which you know stands for 12-decibel Low Pass. It allows low frequencies to pass unaffected, while filtering out high frequencies (any frequencies above the frequency chosen with the Freq slider). So when you turn the Freq slider all the way up, there are no frequencies above that to be filtered. It's wide open.

3. Change the waveform on Oscillator 1 to a Square wave. This should be slightly less grating than the Sawtooth waveform. It's also fun if you know how to play any classic video game music, such as the *Mario Brothers* music (see Figure 1.14).

Figure 1.14

Basic
Subtractor
Square wave,
with no filters
or modulation.

Now that we can hear our naked square wave without any bells and whistles to confuse the issue, we are ready to explore ADSR in the Amp Envelope.

1. By default, the Attack setting on the Amp Envelope is all the way down at 1 (fastest/shortest attack possible). So when you hit a key, you hear sound instantaneously. Please move the Attack slider up to a value of about 69 (a little over halfway). Depress a key on your MIDI keyboard, and you will now hear that the note fades in slowly. Feel free to experiment with different values to get a feel for this.

2. Turn the Attack back down to zero, and also turn Sustain and Release down to zero.

3. Set the Decay to a value of about 50. Not such a long note anymore! If you turn it down even lower (to any value between zero and 20), the note will be so short as to sound like a percussion instrument. I have mine set at 20 right now, and am amusing myself by playing "Popcorn," the whimsical, pioneering electronic dance mega-hit by Gershon Kingsley. This song was originally played on a Moog synthesizer, by the way. (Google this stuff if you don't know about it!)

4. With your Attack still at zero, and your Decay set at 20, turn up your Sustain level to 50. Hold down a key. You will hear the sharp attack and the quick decay, but the decay will no longer fall down all the way to silence. It stops and holds at an intermediate level. Now turn up your Sustain all the way. When you hold down a key, the sound stays at its maximum level until you let go. Theoretically, the Decay setting would still allow the level to fall to the value designated by the Sustain slider, but since the Sustain value is set at maximum, there is no place to fall!

5. With Attack still at zero, Decay at 20, and Sustain at maximum, move the Release slider (which should still be at zero right now) up to a value of 60. Now strike a key and let go. Notice how the note continues to fade out after you release it.

6. Move the Release slider up to maximum. Now hit a note or a chord, and hear it sustain forever (almost)! Before this drives you crazy, turn the Release slider back down. It would eventually fade out after a while, but it takes a long time (see Figure 1.15).

Figure 1.15

Please release me! With the Release slider set at maximum, you can strike a note, then go check your mail and grab a snack and something to drink, and when you come back your note will still be ringing out.

Honestly, in the past I have suffered some confusion regarding this sustain, release, and decay thing. (Attack always seemed pretty straightforward to me.) You may be a quicker learner than I am, but if you could use some further clarification, please try the following exercise, maintaining the settings from the previous exercise.

1. Set Attack and Sustain to zero.

2. Set Decay to 60 and Release to 81.

3. Depress and hold a key until the sound fades completely away; then let go. Even though your Release is set at a value of 81, you should not hear anything after letting go of the key.

4. Strike and let go of a key as quickly as possible. (Just quickly tap it.) If you do it right, you should hear the effect of your Release setting. The note will continue to fade out even though you have let it go (see Figure 1.16).

Figure 1.16

With your Amp Envelope set this way, you can explore the relationship between decay, sustain, and release.

Steps 3 and 4 work the way they do because the Release setting controls the amount of time it takes for the level of a sound to drop to zero *from whatever level it was when you let go of a note*. When you tap and release the note, it hasn't had time for the Decay portion of the envelope to finish. The note has not dropped back down to zero before you let go. So after you let go, the level will fall at a rate determined by the Release value.

You could also turn the Decay setting all the way down, and turn the Sustain all the way up, and still hear the effect of your Release setting.

19

INTIALIZE PATCH/INITIALIZE PARAMETER

By now you are familiar with the fact that any time you create an instance of the Subtractor (or any Reason instrument), it has the Init Patch (its default settings) loaded. No matter what changes you have made or what other patches you have loaded, you can always return to the Init Patch (in other words, you can always re-initialize the Subtractor) either by choosing Initialize Patch from the Edit menu, or by right-clicking (Ctrl-click, Mac) on the edge of the Subtractor and selecting Initialize Patch.

But what if you are halfway into building a deep patch, and you realize you just want to return one individual parameter (like the Master Level) to its default setting, but want to leave everything else as it is? Simply right-click (Ctrl-click, Mac) on the parameter, and you will see it jump back to its default setting.

Filter Envelope

Now, as we learned a little earlier, it is fun to sweep filter frequencies, and I will certainly attest to the fact that it is fun to twiddle knobs with one's bare hands in order to do so. However, it's also nice just to hit a chord and let something happen while you hold it. The Filter Envelope is the first of several features to be discussed that allows you to build some hands-free dynamic sonic action into your patches. It is an ADSR envelope, which also includes a Filter Envelope Amount knob and a Filter Envelope Invert button (see Figure 1.17).

Figure 1.17
In addition to the standard ADSR sliders, the Filter Envelope includes a Filter Envelope Amount knob and a Filter Envelope Invert button.

1. Start with an empty rack, then add reMix and Subtractor. In the Subtractor's Patch Browser window, it should say Init Patch. Please play a few keys on your MIDI keyboard. Notice the percussive attack that is present in the Init Patch.

2. In the Velocity section, turn down F.Env to zero (12 o'clock). You will see the little red light above it turn off. If you strike a few keys now, you will hear the little percussive attack that was there when striking the keys hard has disappeared because velocity (how hard you strike a key) is no longer affecting how much of the Filter Envelope is applied. The Filter Envelope Amt (amount) knob is already at zero, so the Filter Envelope is not being used at the moment.

3. In the Amp Envelope section, turn the Release slider up to 64.

4. Change the filter type of Filter 1 to LP 24 by clicking the Filter 1 Type button.

5. Turn the Filter 1 Frequency slider down to a value of 24. If you play some keys on your MIDI keyboard, you will not hear very much because most of the frequencies are being filtered out now.

6. Turn the Filter Envelope Amount knob all the way to the right (to its maximum value of 127). Now play some keys, and you will hear the sharp attack and short decay of the Filter Envelope affecting the frequency of Filter 1.

7. Adjust the Filter Envelope so that Attack = 99, Decay = 99, Sustain = zero, and Release = 76 (see Figure 1.18).

8. Play and hold a chord on your MIDI keyboard. Now you can do a nice slow filter sweep while keeping both hands on your keyboard!

Figure 1.18
Where would electronica be without the filter sweep? Who would want to live in such a world?

If you want to check yourself on the above exercise, or if you think you might be missing a trick, you can load a patch called SawtoothSwell, which I saved after going through the exercise. It is included on the CD-ROM in the Subtractor Patches folder.

The next exercise demonstrates the function of the Filter Envelope Invert button. Clicking the Filter Envelope Invert button turns the whole Filter Envelope upside down. For instance, the Decay parameter would normally control how fast the frequency of Filter 1 is lowered. When you engage the Filter Envelope Invert button, this is reversed, and the frequency of Filter 1 will actually increase by the same amount at the rate set by the Decay parameter. To hear this in action, please do the following exercise.

1. Start with an empty rack, then add reMix and Subtractor. In the Subtractor's Patch Browser window, it should say Init Patch. This exercise can get a hair loud, so turn down the Subtractor's Master Level slider to about 60.

2. In the Velocity section, turn down F.Env to zero (12 o'clock). You will see the little red light above it turn off.

3. Set Filter 1 so that Freq=20, Resonance=0, and Type=Notch.

4. Click on the Filter 2 Link button and the Filter 2 On/Off button (which will both light up red).

5. Set Filter 2 Frequency to 58 and Filter 2 Resonance to 89.

6. Set the Filter Envelope so that Attack=0, Decay=63, Sustain=0, and Release=0.

7. Set the Filter Envelope Amount (Amt) knob to 28.

8. Play a few notes, and you will hear the instant attack (Filter 1 frequency is at its highest point), followed by the decay (Filter 1 frequency falls at a rate determined by the Filter Envelope Decay slider).

9. Now click on the Filter Envelope Invert button. Play some more, and you will hear that the envelope has indeed been inverted. Now Filter 1 frequency starts at its low point and rises at a rate determined by the Filter Envelope Decay slider (see Figure 1.19).

Figure 1.19

Using the Filter Envelope Invert button.

Mod Envelope

The Mod Envelope is another magical pair of invisible knob-twiddling hands that I have to tell you about. The *Mod* in Mod Envelope is (of course) short for *modulation,* and we know that to modulate in this context simply means to change or adjust a characteristic. So there is a change that is going to take place, such as changing the pitch of an oscillator or the frequency of Filter 2. The degree of this change will be determined by the Mod Envelope Amount (Amt) knob. How that change is implemented over time will be determined once again by an ADSR envelope (see Figure 1.20).

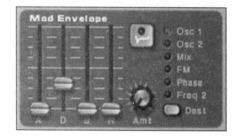

Figure 1.20

The Modulation Envelope, complete with ADSR sliders, Amount knob, Invert button, and Destination selector.

The Mod Envelope looks almost exactly the same as the Filter Envelope. Like the Filter Envelope, it has sliders for Attack, Decay, Sustain, and Release. It also has an Amount knob and an Invert button. However, unlike the Filter Envelope, the Mod Envelope has a Destination button. While the Filter Envelope is hardwired to affect Filter 1 frequency, the Modulation Envelope can be assigned to affect Oscillator 1 pitch, Oscillator 2 pitch, the mix between Osc 1 and Osc 2, the amount of frequency modulation (FM), the phase offset of both Osc 1 and Osc2 (simultaneously), and Filter 2 Frequency. Let's give it a spin. You know the drill by now, but here it goes.

1. Start with an empty rack, then add reMix and Subtractor. In the Subtractor's Patch Browser window, it should say Init Patch.

2. Turn the Mod Envelope Amount (Amt) knob up to 12 o'clock. Play some notes on your MIDI keyboard, and you should hear an immediate effect. By default, the Mod Envelope Destination is set for Osc 1, so the Mod Envelope is affecting the pitch of Osc 1. Since the Mod Envelope Attack is set for 0, the Mod Envelope affects the pitch of Osc 1 immediately to a degree determined by the Mod Envelope Amount knob. The short decay allows the pitch of Osc 1 to fall back to normal quickly, almost like an electronic drum sound.

3. Click the Osc 2 On/Off button so that it is lit red, then click the Mod Envelope Destination (Dest) button until the red light next to FM is lit. Play a few notes, and you will hear the Mod Envelope applied to the FM amount.

4. Click on Filter 2's On/Off button so it is lit up red. Set the Filter 2 Resonance (Res) slider to 99.

5. Select Filter 2 frequency (Freq 2) as the destination for the Mod Envelope (see Figure 1.21). Play your MIDI keyboard to hear the effect.

Figure 1.21
The Modulation Envelope is being applied to Filter 2 frequency.

LFO Section

A low-frequency oscillator is an oscillator that is usually set to oscillate at frequencies well below the bottom range of human hearing, and it is used to modulate another signal at regular intervals. The LFO itself is never heard, only its effect on another signal. Setting the speed on a Chorus effect, Flanger effect, Phase Shifter, or the speed of the Vibrato or Tremolo effect built into a guitar amplifier are all examples of setting the frequency of an LFO. The Subtractor boasts two LFOs, which have different feature sets and applications. Like the Mod Envelope, the LFO section allows you to add some hands-free dramatic motion to a patch.

LFO 1

LFO 1 has six waveforms. It can sync to your track. It is a beautiful thing (see Figure 1.22).

Figure 1.22

LFO 1 has waveforms aplenty, plus it can sync to your track.

Here's the breakdown:

- **Sync**—When this is activated, LFO 1 is automatically synchronized to your track.
- **Rate**—When Sync is not active, this sets the speed of the LFO at any value between zero and 127. When Sync is active, the Rate knob values are note time divisions, ranging from 1/64 to 1/32. Like all the Subtractor parameters, it displays its value when you mouse-click on it.
- **Amount**—The LFO 1 Amount knob sets the amount (or depth) of LFO that will be applied.
- **Destination**—The LFO 1 Dest button selects what will be modulated by LFO 1. The destination choices are as follows:
  - **Osc 1,2**—LFO 1 modulates the pitch of Oscillators 1 and 2 simultaneously.
  - **Osc 2**—LFO 1 modulates the pitch of Oscillator 2 only.
  - **F.Freq**—LFO 1 modulates the frequency of Filter 1.
  - **FM**—LFO 1 modulates the FM amount (the amount by which the frequency of Oscillator 1 is modulated by the frequency of Oscillator 2).

- **Phase**—LFO 1 modulates the degree of phase offset for both Osc 1 and Osc 2 simultaneously.

- **Mix**—LFO 1 modulates the mix (relative output levels) between Osc 1 and Osc 2.

■ **Waveform Selector**—Selects between the following six waveforms.

- **Triangle Wave**—With each cycle, the amplitude of the Triangle wave rises gradually as it approaches its maximum (the peak of the triangle), and then falls gradually at the same rate and to the same degree, making it ideal for vibrato and smooth tremolo effects, as well as siren effects.

- **Inverse Sawtooth**—The Inverse Sawtooth "ramps up," just like the picture.

- **Sawtooth Wave**—The Sawtooth wave starts at the maximum amplitude and then "ramps down."

- **Square Wave**—Unlike the smooth undulation of the Triangle wave, the Square wave alternates sharply between two values.

■ **Random**—This produces a series of random steps. Also known as *sample and hold*, due to the mechanism by which these random steps are traditionally produced. On an analog synthesizer, an input signal (typically from the Noise Generator, due to the random waveforms it produces) is *sampled* when the sample and hold circuit receives a pulse from the internal clock (or other designated trigger signal). In the same instant, the sample and hold circuit sets its output level to the same value as the sampled input level. It will then *hold* that output level until the next trigger pulse comes along, causing the circuit to once again sample and hold the latest input signal value.

■ **Soft Random**—This is the same as Random but with smooth transitions between the steps.

LFO 1 gives us a great chance to make a connection between the sound of these waveforms, the visual representation of the shape of the waveforms, and the names of the waveforms.

The easiest way to "hear the shapes" of these waveforms is to route the output of LFO 1 to modulate the pitch of an oscillator.

1. Start with an empty rack and add reMix and Subtractor. In the Subtractor's Patch Browser window, it should say Init Patch.

2. In the Velocity section, turn down F.Env to zero (12 o'clock). You will see the little red light above it turn off.

3. Turn the Filter 1 Frequency slider up to 90.

4. Change Osc 1 Waveform to a Square wave.

5. Turn the Amp Envelope Decay all the way up to 127. Now you are ready to play.

6. By default, the destination of LFO 1 is set to modulate the pitch of Osc 1 and 2. Turn up the LFO 1 Amount to about 69 and play some notes on your MIDI keyboard. Imagine a bunch of those Triangle waves joined end to end (like a zigzag pattern) and notice that you are hearing that pattern.

25

7. One at a time, select each waveform by clicking the LFO I Waveform Selector button and listen to its shape (see Figure 1.23).

Figure 1.23

Hear the shape, see the waveforms. Suffer from synesthesia much? (See what I'm saying?)

Now let's check out how the Sync feature can be used. You will be applying LFO I to the frequency of Filter I (and Filter 2) this time.

1. Start with an empty rack and add reMix and Subtractor (with its Init Patch).

2. Turn the Amp Envelope Decay all the way up to 127.

3. Set Filter I so that its Freq slider is set to 64 and Resonance is 92. Set the Filter Type to BP 12 (12-Decibel Band Pass).

4. Turn on the Filter 2 Link button and turn on Filter 2.

5. Set Filter 2 Frequency to 48.

6. Set LFO I Destination to F.Freq. Set the Waveform Selector to Random.

7. Turn on the LFO I Sync button so it lights up red. Set LFO I Rate to 1/8 and Amount to 69.

8. Make sure the Click is turned on in the Transport Panel and press Play on the Transport Panel. You should hear your Click ticking away at 120 BPM. Now hold down a note or a chord on your MIDI keyboard, and you will hear LFO I random-stepping the filter frequency in perfect sync to your track tempo (see Figure 1.24).

Figure 1.24

LFO I is random-stepping the frequencies of both filters in perfect sync to the track tempo.

LFO 2

LFO 2 is quite different from LFO 1, and it is also quite useful in its own way (see Figure 1.25). It has only one waveform, which is the Triangle wave. It has knobs for Rate, Amount (or depth), Keyboard Tracking (for increasing the LFO 2 amount as you play higher notes on the keyboard), and Delay (for adding a pause between the time a note is played and the time LFO 2 begins affecting the signal). It can send its modulation signal to four different destinations, depending on which is selected by the LFO 2 Destination button.

Figure 1.25

LFO 2 includes a Keyboard Tracking function (which affects the rate of LFO 2 across the keyboard), as well as a Delay function (so that LFO 2 only begins affecting your signal after you hold down the note for a second or two).

Unlike LFO 1, which has one constant modulation cycle going all the time, LFO 2 triggers another separate modulation cycle with each note played. The following exercise looks at two of the four possible destinations for LFO 2. You will first be modulating the pitch of Oscillator 1 just a bit (for a vibrato effect), and then you will modulate the Amp level to achieve a tremolo effect.

1. Start with an empty rack and add reMix and Subtractor. In the Subtractor's Patch Browser window, it should say Init Patch.

2. Turn the Filter 1 Frequency slider all the way up.

3. Change Osc 1 Waveform to a Sine wave.

4. Change LFO 2 Destination to Osc 1,2.

5. Set LFO 2 Amount to 22, Rate to 78, and Delay to 24. You may be interested to play a few notes before and after each of these three changes, just to check out what's going on. After you press a key, you should hear the note unmodulated for a quick second (the Delay setting) before you hear LFO 2 begin modulating the pitch of Oscillator 1.

6. Change LFO 2 destination to Amp by clicking the Dest button a few times. Now LFO 2 will be modulating the overall volume level of the Subtractor.

7. Set LFO 2 Delay to zero, Rate to 66, and Amount to 75. Play your MIDI keyboard. You should now have a nice tremolo effect (see Figure 1.26). I have saved this under the name SineTremelo in the Subtractor Patches folder on the included CD-ROM.

Figure 1.26

LFO 2 is great for adding tasty tremolo and vibrato effects to your patches.

Of course, you should now be getting familiar enough with the Subtractor to be able to imagine routing LFO 2 to Filter 2 Frequency or to Osc 1 and 2 Phase Offset. In fact, you will be routing LFO 2 to Osc 1 and 2 Phase Offset in an advanced patch at the end of this chapter.

Play Parameters

The following parameters deal primarily with the Subtractor's reaction to how you play your MIDI controller. They also define how the Subtractor reacts to modulation messages from a standard MIDI controller.

Velocity

Velocity in this context means how hard you hit the keys on your MIDI keyboard (or how hard you strike the pads if you have a Trigger Finger or similar MIDI drum pad device). There are a whopping nine parameters which can be affected by how hard you play. Each parameter has a knob that determines to what extent the parameter is positively or negatively affected by velocity (see Figure 1.27), as explained in the following list.

■ **Amp**—This controls the overall volume of the Subtractor. When turned off (knob at 12 o'clock), every note plays at the same volume, no matter how hard you strike it. Turning the knob to the right of center means the harder you play, the louder it sounds. Turning it to the left of center will result in the opposite, with higher velocities producing quieter sounds.

28

■ **FM**—Turning this knob to the right of center will result in higher FM Amount values the harder you play. Turning it left of center will result in lower FM Amount values the harder you play. This setting has no effect unless either Osc 2 or the Noise Generator are active.

■ **Mod Envelope (M.Env)**—Turning this knob to the right of center results in higher Mod Envelope Amount values the harder you play. Turning it to the left of center results in lower Mod Envelope Amount values the harder you play.

■ **Phase**—This adjusts the Phase Offset value for both Osc 1 and Osc 2, depending on how hard you play. It will retain the relative offset values between the two Phase Offset knobs in the Oscillator section. Turning this knob to the right of center results in greater Phase Offset values the harder you play, and turning it to the left of center results in lower Phase Offset values the harder you play.

■ **Freq 2**—Turning this knob to the right of center will result in higher Filter 2 Frequency values the harder you play. Turning left of center will result in lower Filter 2 Frequency values the harder you play.

■ **Filter Envelope (F.Env)**—Turning this knob to the right results in higher Filter Envelope Amount values the harder you play. Turning it to the left results in lower Filter Envelope Amount values the harder you play.

■ **Filter Envelope Decay (F.Dec)**—Turning this knob to the right means that the harder you play, the longer the Filter Envelope Decay will be. Turning it to the left means that the harder you play, the shorter the Filter Envelope Decay will be.

■ **Mix**—Turning this knob to the right of center will result in more of Osc 2 being present in the mix the harder you play. Turning the knob left of center will result in more of Osc 1 being present in the mix the harder you play.

■ **Amp Envelope Attack (A.Atk)**—Turning this knob to the right means that the harder you play, the longer the Amp Envelope Attack will be. Turning it to the left means that the harder you play, the shorter the Amp Envelope Attack will be.

Figure 1.27
How hard you play can affect up to nine different parameters in the Subtractor.

Pitch Bend

The Pitch Bend wheel corresponds to the pitch bend on your MIDI keyboard, and can also be controlled with your mouse or with automation in the Reason Sequencer (see Figure 1.28). Above the

Pitch Bend wheel is the Pitch Bend Range control, with which you can select an extra-large bend range of up to +/−24 steps (two octaves). You could do some pretty violent pitch bending with such a wide range.

Pitch Bend has several applications. For example, it can be used to simulate string bends when using electric guitar patches. Setting the bend range to a value of two steps can result in more natural and harmonically satisfying bends in that case. Pitch Bend is also great for synth lead sounds, where wider bend ranges can produce wilder effects. You can also use the Pitch Bend wheel to "cheat" and transpose on the spot. So if you are not actually quite at Herbie Hancock's level with your keyboard skills, you can keep playing in your comfortable key and instantly transpose whatever you are playing by moving your Pitch Bend wheel all the way up or down.

Modulation Wheel

When you catch on to what I'm about to tell you regarding the Modulation wheel destination assignment, you are going to be asking, "Man, why didn't you tell me this before, back when I was using my mouse to sweep all those filter frequencies and FM amounts!" That's right: You could have been using the Mod wheel on your MIDI keyboard instead.

The Modulation wheel can control any combination of the following parameters: Filter 1 Frequency, Filter 1 Resonance, LFO 1 Amount, Phase Offset (for both Osc 1 and 2 simultaneously), and FM Amount. Each of these parameters will be either positively or negatively affected by turning up the Mod wheel, depending on the position of the +/− knob next to the parameter name (see Figure 1.28).

Figure 1.28
The Pitch Bend wheel has an assignable range of up to 24 semitones, while the Modulation wheel can be assigned to control any combination of up to five Subtractor parameters.

Legato/ReTrig Mode

How the Subtractor Envelopes are triggered by MIDI note on/off information is determined by the Legato/ReTrig Mode button (see Figure 1.29). Following are descriptions of the two available trigger modes.

Figure 1.29
The Legato/ReTrig Mode button.

- **Legato Mode**—The effect of Legato mode is most easily heard with monophonic patches (Polyphony set to 1). If you strike a note without first letting go of the previous note, the Envelopes will not be retriggered. You will not hear a new attack until you first release all notes before hitting the next.

- **ReTrig Mode**—When the ReTrig mode is selected, the Subtractor's Envelopes are triggered each time you play a note, even if you are still holding down other notes. If the patch you are playing is monophonic (Polyphony set to 1), then if you hold down one note, play a second note while still holding down the first, and then release the second note while still holding down the first, the first note will trigger the Envelopes again when you release the second note.

Portamento

No, this is not a Franken-food cross between a portabella and a pimento. It's a smooth way to get from one note to another. Normally, when you hit one note and then another, the pitch jumps immediately from one note to the next. If you turn up the Portamento knob (see Figure 1.30), you are increasing the time it takes to "glide" from one note to the next.

Figure 1.30
Portamento controls the amount of time it takes to smoothly "glide" from one note to another.

This effect can be heard on the long synth solo at the end of Emerson, Lake, and Palmer's "Lucky Man." Or it can be heard right now in your home studio. Give it a try. It's kinda fun! With the Portamento knob turned up, the effect is most noticeable when you play a very low note on the keyboard and then play a very high one (or vice-versa). This effect can be good for simulating vintage Theremin sounds, especially if you also use an LFO to add a bit of Triangle wave modulation to your Oscillator 1 and 2 frequency.

Low Bandwidth

Oh, please! The Low Bandwidth button is supposed to save a bit of CPU power, at the expense of removing just a little high-end definition from your Subtractor patches. Perhaps this is not very noticeable (especially on bass patches), but if your CPU is scared of a little old Subtractor, it's time to take it out back and shoot it and get a *real* computer.

I generally want the highest quality sound I can get, therefore I have no use for a "makes it sound slightly worse" button. I never touch the Low BW button (see Figure 1.31).

Figure 1.31

The vestigial organ known as the Low Bandwidth button. Probably left over from the first versions of Reason when computers were not as fast and perhaps a few Subtractors could add up to more of a challenge.

Polyphony

This, very simply, determines how many notes you can play at one time. Sometimes, it's nice to set it at 1 (monophonic) for bass sounds and for shredding classic lead sounds. When the Polyphony is set at 1, the most recent note you have touched will be the one you hear, even if you are holding down another note. This allows you to do some "hammer-on," or *pivot* effects.

To hear what I'm talking about, set your Polyphony to 1, and while you are holding down one note, strike another key over and over again. Monophonic playing can sound "cleaner" than higher Polyphony settings when playing fast because you will only hear one note at a time, even if you accidentally hit two notes at the same time. If you set the Polyphony to a value higher than 1, the note priority will be handled in the following way. If you set your Polyphony to 4 (for example), and then play a five-note chord, bringing in one note at a time, the first note of the chord will cut off once the fifth note is played. Whenever you attempt to play a number of simultaneous notes that exceeds the polyphony setting, the least recently played notes will be cut off in favor of the most recently played notes (see Figure 1.32).

Figure 1.32

The Polyphony setting determines how many notes you can be playing at one time.

External Modulation

The Subtractor can receive additional modulation from your MIDI controller, provided your MIDI controller is so equipped. If your MIDI keyboard has aftertouch, or an expression pedal jack, or if you have a MIDI breath controller, these MIDI messages can be used to control any combination of the following parameters: Filter 1 Frequency, LFO1 Amount, Amp Level, and FM Amount. Each of these parameters will be either positively or negatively affected by an external modulation signal to an extent determined by the position of the +/− knob next to the parameter name. Which sort of external modulation message is to be received is determined by the External Mod Select button (see Figure 1.33).

It's pretty nice to be able to sweep the filter frequency by moving an expression pedal or by applying pulsating pressure to a chord while you are holding it.

Figure 1.33

The External Modulation feature allows the use of an expression pedal,
a breath controller, or aftertouch to modulate various Subtractor parameters.

Control Voltage Routing

Control voltage routing in Reason is obviously used as a concept, since you are only connecting virtual cables and there are only calculations of emulated control voltage. If you are unfamiliar with analog synthesizers, you may wonder why the concept is even included.

In an analog synthesizer, everything is controlled by electricity. If the Subtractor were an analog synthesizer, each one of its oscillators would be a voltage-controlled oscillator (VCO). Applying different control voltages to a VCO will result in the VCO producing different pitches (oscillating at different frequencies). The analog synthesizer will have voltage-controlled filters (VCF) and voltage-controlled amplifiers (VCA). Apply more control voltage to the VCA, and your audio signal will become louder. This can be aptly compared to the way applying more air pressure in a wind instrument produces a louder sound.

Just about every device in Reason has routing for control voltage. In this way, you can directly affect the behavior of one device with control voltages produced by one or more other devices.

Hit the Tab key on your computer keyboard to flip your Reason rack around, and take a look at the back of the Subtractor (see Figure 1.34). Check out all those holes! In the upper-right corner you will find the Subtractor's single audio output. Every other jack on the back of the Subtractor is designed to emulate a control voltage (CV) input or output. Just when you thought we'd pretty much covered every inch of the Subtractor!

The Subtractor's CV inputs and outputs are grouped into four sections: Sequencer Control, Modulation Input, Modulation Output, and Gate Input.

■ **Sequencer Control**—These inputs allow the Subtractor to be played by external CV instead of by MIDI input. Examples would be the CV output of the Matrix or of Redrum. Monophonic sources will work best. The Gate input receives note on/off and velocity information, while the CV input receives pitch information.

■ **Modulation Input**—The Modulation Input section includes CV inputs for Osc Pitch (controls both Osc 1 and 2 pitch simultaneously), Osc Phase (controls both Osc 1 and 2 Phase Offset simultaneously), FM Amount, Filter 1 Frequency, Filter 1 Resonance, Filter 2 Frequency, Amp Level, and Mod wheel. Each of these inputs has a Voltage Trim knob to its left, which can be used to boost or attenuate the incoming control voltage.

■ **Modulation Output**—This section sends control voltage outputs from the Subtractor's Modulation Envelope, from the Filter Envelope, and from LFO 1. These modulation sources can modulate external devices at the same time that they modulate Subtractor parameters internally.

■ **Gate Input**—Instead of triggering the Subtractor's Envelopes the normal way (by playing notes into the Subtractor), the Envelopes can also be triggered by external control voltages. Once you connect one of these Gate inputs to a CV source, the corresponding Envelope will no longer be triggered by notes you play on your keyboard or within your MIDI sequence. But you will not hear anything unless notes are being played, since envelopes do nothing if there is no signal to shape. The three Subtractor Envelopes that can be triggered by external control voltage are the Amp Envelope, the Filter Envelope, and the Mod Envelope.

We will get into some serious CV routing in Chapter 5, "The Combinator," in which we will explore how the Reason instruments can interact with each other, merging into giant mutant monster instruments!

Figure 1.34

The Subtractor's control voltage inputs and outputs are grouped into four sections: Sequencer Control, Modulation Input, Modulation Output, and Gate Input.

WHAT HAPPENNED TO MY BRILLIANT CV ROUTING?

It is important to note that any CV connections you make will NOT be saved with the Subtractor Patch, even if the connections are to and from the same Subtractor. The good news is, if that Subtractor is inside of a Combinator, you can make CV connections galore and they will all be saved with the Combinator patch. You will learn all about this in Chapter 5, "TheCombinator."

Your First Advanced Subtractor Patch

Your first advanced Subtractor patch is going to be a weird one. Why not? There are plenty of perfectly normal patches in the Reason Factory Sound Bank ReFill. This patch is going to build on what you learned in the "Ring Modulation" section of this chapter. It is going to result in an inharmonic pad, which could be suitable for some otherworldly sound design project.

1. Start with an empty rack and then add reMix and Subtractor (with the Init Patch loaded).

2. In the Velocity section, turn down F.Env to zero (12 o'clock). You will see the little red light above it turn off.

3. Turn Filter 1's Freq slider up to 87 and make sure that the Filter Type is set to LP 12.

4. Set up your Amp Envelope so that Attack = 81, Decay = 100, Sustain = 64, and Release = 79.

4. Set the Waveform of Osc 1 to Sine wave. Then set Osc 1 Octave to 6 and Semi to 11.

5. Turn on Osc 2 by clicking on its little red power button and set the Waveform of Osc 2 to a Triangle wave. Then turn off Osc 2 Keyboard Tracking. This way the (unheard) carrier signal will be the same frequency, no matter what note you play on your keyboard.

6. Turn the Mix knob all the way to the right so that Osc 1 (your input or modulation signal) cannot be heard. The frequency of Osc 2 (the carrier signal) will be modulated by the frequency of Osc 1.

7. Click the Ring Mod power button so it lights up red. Play a chord (any chord, since this patch is inharmonic) and listen to the sound fade in, thanks to the long Attack setting in the Amp Envelope.

8. Now let's bring in the second layer of strangeness. Set your Mod Envelope so that Attack = 91, Decay = 96, Sustain = zero, and Release = 81. Set the Amount knob to 48 and set the Mod Envelope Destination to FM so that the Mod Envelope modulates the FM amount. Play a chord, and you will hear the effect of the FM fading in just after the original Ring Modulated tone fades in. If you continue holding down the chord, you will hear the effect of the FM fade out again as the Decay portion of the Mod Envelope runs its course.

9. I like the way this sounds right now, but just in case you need it to get even weirder, let's look at LFO 1. Use the LFO 1 Waveform Selector button to choose Random (the fifth one down) and leave the LFO 1 Destination set for Osc 1,2. Set LFO 1 Rate to 90. You will not hear any change because you are leaving the LFO 1 Amount knob at zero.

10. Next to the Mod wheel in the lower-left corner of the Subtractor, turn LFO 1 Mod wheel Amount knob to the right so that it has a value of 37. Now when you play a chord, you have the option of easing up your Mod wheel until you can hear the madness of LFO 1 modulating the pitch of Osc 1 and 2 with a Random waveform (see Figure 1.35).

Figure 1.35

Your ringmodFMswell patch should look like this when you're done.

11. Don't forget to save your patch by clicking the little diskette icon to the far right of the Subtractor Patch Browser. For your reference, a version of this patch has been saved on the CD-ROM included with this book. It is located in the Subtractor Patches folder and is named ringmodFMswell.

By the way, although I did not include any Portamento in my example patch, the ringmodFMswell patch sounds really sick with some high Portamento values (very slow Portamento).

Advanced Subtractor Patch II

This next patch is not as strange as the previous one, but it has some delightful complexity in its behavior, and it's also rather pretty. This patch includes modulation of the Phase Offset of Oscillators 1 and 2, as well as modulation of the Frequency Modulation amount.

1. Start with an empty rack and add reMix and Subtractor. In the Subtractor's Patch Browser window, it should say Init Patch.

2. Turn the Filter 1 Frequency slider all the way up.

3. Change Osc 1 and Osc 2 Waveforms to Sine wave.

4. Change LFO2 Destination to Osc 1,2.

5. Set LFO 2 Destination to Phase. Now LFO 2 is modulating the phase sffset of both Osc 1 and Osc 2.

6. Set LFO 2 Rate to 46, Amount to 127, Keyboard Track to 25 (so that the higher keys modulate a little faster than the lower keys), and leave the Delay set at zero.

7. Turn on Osc 2 and set the Phase modes of both oscillators to Waveform Subtraction (–). Play a chord or two, and you should hear a gentle chorus-like sound as LFO 2 modulates the phase sffset of Osc 1 and 2.

8. Turn up the FM Amount to 26 and turn down Osc 2 Phase Offset all the way to the left. Play a bit with long, sustained multiple notes. Because each note in LFO 2 triggers another LFO cycle, and also because a higher LFO Rate is being applied to the higher keys than the lower keys (thanks to the LFO 2 Keyboard Tracking setting), all these notes you are playing will be pulsing at different rates. This can result in a complex, gentle, and abstract rhythmic content in the sound.

9. Now set up the Modulation Envelope so that Amount = 46, Attack = 99, Decay = 99, Sustain = zero, and Release = 99. Set the Mod Envelope Destination to FM. Play some long, sustained chords, bringing different notes in and out as you do and listening to all the different rhythmic patterns of pulsation. You will hear what sounds like a slow filter sweep as the Mod Envelope slowly modulates the FM amount. Please try this in all registers of the keyboard, as it sounds quite different depending on which octave you are playing in. By the way, I turned my Polyphony up to 10 for this one, so I can use all my fingers!

10. Don't forget to save your patch by clicking the diskette icon to the far right of the Subtractor Patch Browser (see Figure 1.36). For your reference, a version of this patch has been saved on the CD-ROM included with this book. It is located in the Subtractor Patches folder and is named PhaseArp.

Figure 1.36

Your PhaseArp patch should look like this when you're done.

CHECK YOUR WORK

As you go through the tutorials in this chapter you may find yourself wondering, "Is it supposed to sound like this?" With this book, it is easy to check your work. Finished patches, as well as examples of some of the patches being used in Reason song files, can be found on the CD included with this book.

I hope that by now you have made friends with the Subtractor and are starting to feel at home with synthesis in general. In the next chapter, you can apply that knowledge to a completely different virtual synthesizer: the Malström! You will find some familiar ground there (thanks to the work you've done in this chapter), but you will also find that the Malström has all sorts of new tricks up its sleeve.

2   The Malström

While Subtractor should seem fairly straightforward and familiar to people accustomed to working with analog synthesizers, the Malström has some features which may have vintage analog synth users scratching their heads for a minute or two (see Figure 2.1). That is actually a good thing because it means you get to create sound in some novel and ear-catching ways. Though the design of this synth is quite original and therefore perhaps a bit unfamiliar, the number of controls is finite, and their operation is logical. We will go through them one step at a time, hanging out at each stop along the way as long as necessary for you to fully grasp every function and make it your own.

Figure 2.1
The Malström is a wholly original creation from Propellerhead, unlike any other synth on the planet.

The Malström: A Different Kind of Synth

The Malström uses a form of synthesis called *Graintable synthesis*. This method is a combination of *granular synthesis* and *wavetable synthesis*. Before moving further into the Malström's parameters, it is appropriate to briefly and generally discuss granular and wavetable synthesis, as well as explain how they are combined to create the Graintable synthesis with which the Malström produces its sound.

39

Granular synthesis uses thousands of extremely short audio segments (called *grains*), which are combined to form a larger audio event. These grains (which can be as small as only a few milliseconds each) can be derived from an audio sample or can be derived mathematically. The overall sound produced by these combined grains (sometimes referred to as a *grain cloud)* can be changed by altering various individual properties of each grain or by altering properties of the overall grain cloud (including its density, as well as the order in which the grains occur). This results in a complex (often quite weird or fantastic) and infinitely variable soundscape that makes granular synthesis a truly unique process in the world of sound design.

Wavetable synthesis is based on the playback and manipulation of several digital samples of single wave cycles, which are referenced in a list called a *wavetable*. It is possible to sweep though a wavetable at various speeds (and in any sequential or non-sequential order) without affecting the pitch of the waves. It is also possible to isolate and loop specific waves referenced within the wavetable. Because wavetable synthesis makes use of sampled waveforms, sounds with a high degree of realism can be produced. And since a single wavetable may contain all sorts of wildly different waveforms, the abililty to jump back and forth between them (and interpolate the spaces in between) within a single patch can make for some creative and unique sonic textures.

To generate a sound using the Malström's Graintable synthesis technique, a sampled sound is processed and cut up into a number of grains, varying in length between 5 and 100 milliseconds. When these grains are spliced back together into a linear sequence, the result is a *Graintable*, which can be swept through just like a wavetable at any speed without affecting pitch. The Malström's Graintable synthesis also allows other nifty tricks, including the ability to resize the individual grains within a Graintable.

As we move on into the Malström's parameters, it is worth remembering that although the Malström uses Graintable synthesis for the generation of the initial stage of its sound, it also uses subtractive synthesis (like the Subtractor) to shape its sound. Subtracting overtones using the Malström's filters is an example of subtractive synthesis at work within the Malström. The Malström also makes use of a third variety of synthesis called *waveshaping synthesis*, which you will get to hear in action when you use the Malström's Shaper feature later in this chapter.

Oscillator Section

If you are coming from an analog synthesizer background, it may seem a bit confusing to use the word *oscillator* in this context. Something like "sound generator" might be more intuitive. Rather than emulating an analog oscillator circuit, which produces a constant, relatively simple waveform (like the Subtractor's oscillators do), the Malström's Oscillator section generates its sound by playing back Graintables (as discussed in the previous section).

Within a patch, each of the two Malström oscillators will do two things: play back a Graintable and generate a pitch. In contrast, the Subtractor's Oscillator section emulates analog voltage-controlled oscillators, which generate a constant signal whose pitch will only be varied according to which key is being played if you engage the Keyboard Tracking feature, which, in turn, emulates sending a different control voltage to the VCO (voltage-controlled oscillator), depending on which key you play. If this varying control voltage is not applied to the Oscillator, the pitch you hear stays the same no matter what key you play. Not so with the Malström. The pitch of its oscillators is always dependent on which key you play. There is no Keyboard Tracking feature to turn on or off in the Oscillator section of the Malström (see Figure 2.2).

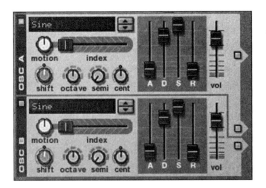

Figure 2.2

The Oscillator section of the Malström.

Both Osc A and Osc B have the same controls, although their output routing is a bit different. The following controls are identical for both oscillators:

- **Oscillator On/Off**—Each of the Malström's two oscillators has its own On/Off button in the upper-left corner of the oscillator.

- **Amp Envelope**—Each of the Malström's two oscillators has its own Amplitude Envelope, with sliders for Attack, Decay, Sustain, and Release. For an in-depth discussion on ADSR and Amp Envelopes, please refer to Chapter 1, "The Subtractor." Though the function of the ADSR Amp Envelope is the same, Malstrom's inclusion of separate Amp Envelopes for each Oscillator provides an additional level of flexibility not available on the Subtractor.

- **Oscillator Volume**—Each of the Malström's two oscillators has its own Volume slider.

- **Graintable Selector**—Selects from a long list of over 80 Graintables available for use within the Malström. Although they can be selected with the up/down arrows to the right of the Graintable Display window, you might prefer to click on the window itself because this will open a pop-up menu that shows all the available Graintables at once; you can then click on the one you want (see Figure 2.3). Since much of the complexity of the Malström's patches comes from the Graintables themselves, I encourage you to simply create an instance of the Malström, and then try all the different Graintables in Oscillator A. By default, there is no extra processing being applied to these Graintables in a freshly initialized Malström, so you can hear them by themselves with no subsequent filtering or modulation.

- **Octave**—Alters the pitch of the Graintable up to +/− seven octaves.

- **Semi**—Alters the pitch of the Graintable up to +/− 12 semitones (one octave).

- **Cent**—Fine-tunes the pitch of the Graintable up to +/− 100 cents (one semitone).

- **Index**—This slider selects the specific point in the Graintable at which playback will start when a note is played. The sequence of grains in the Graintable from start to finish corresponds to values from left to right on the Index slider. So when the Index slider is all the way to the left, the first grain (or segment) of the Graintable will also be played first when the Malström receives a Note On message. The correspondence is not point for point, however; like every MIDI parameter, there are only 128 possible values for the Index slider (0–127), but the number of grains in a given Graintable may be less than or greater than 128.

- **Motion**—The setting of the Motion knob determines how quickly the oscillator will move from one grain in the Graintable to the next. Set at a value of zero (12 o'clock), the selected Graintable will playback at its default speed. Setting the Motion knob to a position right of center will result in a Graintable that plays back increasingly more quickly than its default speed, the farther right you turn the knob. Setting the Motion knob to the left of center will result in playback that is increasingly slower than the default for a selected Graintable the farther left you turn the knob. If the Motion knob is all the way to the left (at its minimum setting), then there will be no motion at all. This means that the oscillator will never move from the first grain (designated by the Index slider), and the oscillator will simply loop this initial grain over and over again, without ever playing back any of the other grains.

- **Shift**—The Shift knob adjusts the overall harmonic character of the sound by adjusting the size of the individual grains in the selected Graintable. The Shift knob is bipolar, so the default setting of 12 o'clock represents a Shift value of zero, which means you will hear the default grain size for the selected Graintable. Setting the Shift knob to the left will result in larger grain sizes, and turning the knob to the right of center will result in smaller grain sizes. For more on this, please refer to the "Shift: A Closer Look" section a little later on in this chapter.

Index: A Closer Look

The first Oscillator section parameter I would like to draw your attention to is the Index slider. The following brief exercise should give you a feel for the function of the Index slider.

1. Create an instance of the Malström. The Initialization Patch will be loaded by default.

2. Click on the Oscillator A Graintable Display window (so that you see the long vertical pop-up menu) and select FX: Thunder. Hold down the C2 key on your MIDI keyboard to hear what this Graintable sounds like. (If you are having trouble figuring out which key is C2, just find a key that sounds appropriately thunderous.) Notice how there is an initial higher-pitched "thunder burst" at the beginning of the sound, followed by a lower rolling thunder sound that eventually fades into the distance until the oscillator loops back to the beginning of the Graintable, and you hear the initial thunder burst again. Let go of the C2 key.

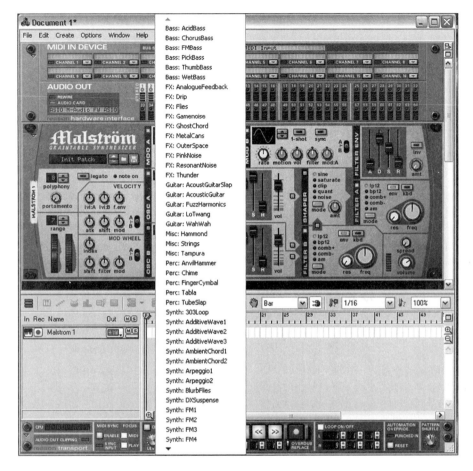

Figure 2.3

Clicking on the Graintable Display window opens a pop-up menu from which you can select one of over 80 Graintables.

3. Now move the Oscillator A Index slider about 1/3 of the way to the left (to a value of about 43 or so). Hold down the C2 key again. This time you will not hear the initial higher-pitched thunder burst at the beginning because you chose a start point (with the Index slider) later in the Graintable, after the initial thunder burst had already occurred. If you continue holding down the key, then you will hear the Graintable loop back and play the beginning of the Graintable, thunder burst and all. You can experiment with different Index settings to hear the Graintable begin playing back at different start points (see Figure 2.4).

Figure 2.4

The Index slider is used to select the specific point in the Graintable at which playback will start when a note is played.

43

Notice that the FX: Thunder Graintable is programmed with a *forward motion pattern*, which means it plays from the start of the Graintable to the end and then starts over again. Some other Malström Graintables are programmed with a forward/backward motion pattern, which means the Graintable will play from beginning to end and then backward from end to beginning; it will keep repeating this way as long as you hold the key down. The motion pattern is programmed into the Graintable itself and cannot be changed.

Motion: A Closer Look

Now let's take a look at the Motion knob (see Figure 2.5). Please do not confuse this with the *motion pattern*, which cannot be adjusted. The Motion knob controls the speed at which the oscillator sweeps through the grains of the selected Graintable. The default position of the Motion knob is at 12 o'clock, which will correspond to the default Motion setting of the selected Graintable. At Motion settings to the right of center, the Graintable will play back more quickly. At settings to the left of center, the Graintable will play back more slowly. If you turn the Motion knob all the way to the left, there will be no Motion at all, and the oscillator will never move from whichever grain is the first one to play, as set by the Index slider. It will just keep playing that single grain over and over again. The following brief exercise should give you a feel for the function of the Motion knob.

Figure 2.5

The Motion knob is used to specify how quickly the oscillator will move from one grain in the Graintable to the next (that is, how quickly the oscillator will sweep through the Graintable).

1. Create an instance of the Malström. The Initialization Patch will be loaded by default.

2. Click on the Oscillator A Graintable Selector window and (once again) select FX: Thunder. Hold down the C2 key on your MIDI keyboard to hear what this sounds like, then let go of the C2 key.

3. Now move the Oscillator A Motion knob all the way to the left. Press the C2 key on your MIDI keyboard again, and you will hear very little because the first grain in this Graintable contains very little audio information. This Thunder sound fades in, so the first grain is almost silent. With the Motion knob set all the way to the left (its minimum setting), there is no motion whatsoever, so Oscillator A will continue playing whatever single grain is specified by the position of the Index slider.

4. Continue holding down the C2 key and sweep the Oscillator A Index slider from left to right. You are now controlling the playback of the Graintable directly, kind of like moving a record forward and backward with the turntable motor disengaged.

5. If you continue holding down the C2 key, but let go of the Index slider (somewhere in the middle of its travel path), the turntable comparison breaks down. When you leave a needle on a stopped record, you don't hear anything! But when you continue to trigger an oscillator that is stopped on one grain, it keeps playing that grain over and over again. Even though the Thunder sound has no discernable pitch when you play the whole Graintable back at the proper speed, an individual grain does have a pitch you can hear (when you loop the grain, that is).

6. Now turn the Oscillator 1 Motion knob up to about −20 and hold down a note. It sounds a bit more suggestive of thunder (if you use your imagination), but you can still hear a definite pitch very clearly. This is because the slow Motion setting still stays on one grain (playing it over and over) for a little while before moving on to the next grain in the Graintable.

7. Continue holding down the C2 key as you sweep the Motion knob to the right. As you approach the center setting, you will no longer be able to discern a pitch; and as you turn the Motion knob all the way to the right, the Thunder Graintable will loop faster and faster until it gets pretty ridiculous.

Shift: A Closer Look

When you adjust the Shift knob, resampling is used to adjust the size of the individual grains in the selected Graintable. This results in an often dramatic adjustment in the harmonic character of the Graintable.

One noticeable effect of changing the size of the individual grains in the Graintable with the Shift control is that specific harmonic frequencies can be very clearly heard as you slowly move the Shift knob from left to right, especially at values right of center. Let's check out a quick example.

1. Create an instance of the Malström. The Initialization Patch will be loaded by default.

2. By default, the Oscillator A Graintable Selector window should display Sine. Click the Graintable Selector Up arrow once to select Sawtooth*4. Note that if you click the Graintable Display window instead to reveal the complete list of Graintables, this Graintable will show up as Wave: Sawtooth*4.

3. Hold down a note or chord in the middle register of your MIDI keyboard. Move the Oscillator A Shift knob slowly from its default center position all the way to the right and listen to the upward harmonic sweep as the grain size is made smaller and smaller.

4. Making the grains larger than default can have an unpredictable effect. Now slowly sweep the Oscillator A Shift knob all the way to the left and hear the Sawtooth*4 Graintable descend into chaos (see Figure 2.6).

Figure 2.6

The Shift knob is used to adjust the size of the individual grains in the selected Graintable.

With some Graintables, you may hear a noticeable change in pitch as you sweep the Shift knob, again, especially at values right of center. With the same Malström instance as used in the previous exercise, set the Oscillator A Shift knob back to 12 o'clock and select the Voice: TibetanMonks Graintable. Hold down a note and slowly sweep the Oscillator A Shift knob all the way to the right. You will hear the perceived pitch go way up.

Another possible effect of changing the size of the individual grains with the Shift knob is an adjustment in the *formant* of the overall sound. The *American Heritage Dictionary* defines *formant* as "any of several frequency regions of relatively great intensity in a sound spectrum, which together determine the characteristic quality of a vowel sound." Sweeping the Shift value sweeps the formant, or prevailing vowel sound, of the selected Graintable, not unlike the way one adjusts the formant of a musical sound by adjusting how one holds one's mouth while playing a Jew's harp, or the position of a Harmon mute over the bell of a trumpet, or the position of a wah-wah pedal under the foot of a guitarist. Vowel sound is often referred to when talking about certain types of filtering or sound-shaping. If you would like to hear a clear example of a shifting formant, create a fresh instance of the Malström, click on the Oscillator A Graintable Selector window (so that you see the long vertical pop-up menu), and select Voice: Formant Saw. The formant shift is built in to the Graintable, so all you have to do to hear the effect is to hold down a key on your MIDI keyboard. OOOOAAAEEEEAAAOOOOAAAEEEAAOO!

The following exercise will demonstrate how the formant of a Graintable can be adjusted by using the Shift knob. In this exercise, you will actually be making the grains of the Graintable larger than their default size in order to achieve the desired effects.

1. Create an instance of the Malström. The Initialization Patch will be loaded by default.

2. Click on the Oscillator A Graintable Selector window (so that you see the long vertical pop-up menu) and select Voice: FemaleChoir. Find a nice chord in the female vocal register. The formant should be an "ahh" sound.

3. Now select an Oscillator A Shift value of about −35. This should result in a formant close to an "oooo" sound.

4. Change the Oscillator A Shift value to −15. You should now have an "oh" sound (see Figure 2.7).

There are many more radical effects you will find as you experiment with applying the Shift parameter to different Graintables.

Figure 2.7

Can I buy a vowel? With this Shift setting, your virtual female choir should be singing "ohhh."

PARAMETER VALUE TOOL TIP: REASON'S BUILT-IN CHEAT SHEET

Mouse over any parameter in any Reason device, and you will see a red box that tells you the full name of the parameter, as well as its current value. This is a very helpful feature, not only because it allows you to see exact parameter values, but also because it gives more specific parameter descriptions than the actual labels on the user interface, which can be a great quick reference.

If you happen to notice that these Tool Tips are *not* popping up when you mouse over parameters, check the General page of the Reason preferences and make sure there is a check mark next to Show Parameter Value Tool Tip. Then you will be sure to receive that extra little measure of help Reason is designed to provide to you (see Figure 2.8).

Figure 2.8

Parameter Value Tool Tip is your ever-present friend. It should always be turned on in your Reason Preferences.

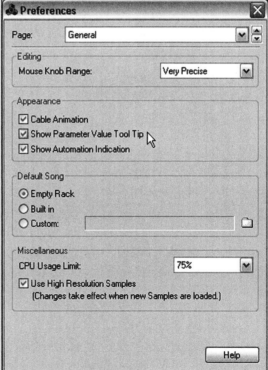

Filter Section

The Malström has a rather unique Filter section (see Figure 2.9). It includes two filters that each include High Pass and Band Pass filters, as well as the novel addition of Comb Filters and AM Filters. Either or both of the filters can be controlled with the Malström's single Filter Envelope. In addition to all this, the Malström includes the Shaper, which is actually capable of modifying the wave shape of the signal being applied to the Shaper input, adding new levels of complexity to the sound.

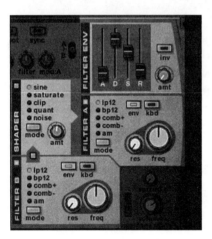

Figure 2.9

The Malström's Filter section has several unique features that can help you shape your sound creatively.

Filters A and B

Visually, the Malström may not immediately suggest symmetry of design. But it does have a level of symmetry not present in the Subtractor. As you read a moment ago, the Malström Oscillators A and B are identical to each other (aside from their output routing). Here again in the Filter section, routing aside, the Malström's Filter A and Filter B are identical and can both be controlled by the same Filter Envelope. Both Malström filters have the following identically arranged controls:

- **Env (Envelope)**—When the Filter Envelope button is engaged, the Freq (Cutoff Frequency) will be modulated by the Malström's ADSR Filter Envelope.

- **Kbd (Keyboard Tracking)**—When the Keyboard Tracking button is engaged, the Freq (Cutoff Frequency) value will increase or decrease, depending on which MIDI notes are being played. Higher keys will result in higher Cutoff Frequency values, and keys in the low range of the keyboard will result in lower Cutoff Frequency values.

- **Freq (Cutoff Frequency)**—This control really has different functions depending on which Filter mode is selected. It sets the cutoff frequency for the LP 12 and BP 12 filters. It sets the delay time for the Comb filters (which does also change the frequency characteristics of the Comb filters). For the AM filter (which is really a Ring Modulator), it sets the frequency of the carrier signal.

■ **Res (Resonance)**—Like the Freq knob, the Resonance knob has different functions depending on which Filter mode is selected. When the LP 12 (12-dB Low Pass) filter is selected, the Resonance knob emphasizes the Cutoff Frequency, causing a sharp resonant spike at the frequency set by the Freq knob. When the BP 12 (12-dB Band Pass) filter is selected, the Resonance knob determines the bandwidth. Lower Resonance settings result in a wider bandwidth (the group or *band* of frequencies that will be allowed to *pass* through the filter), while higher Resonance settings will result in a narrower bandwidth. For the Comb filters, the Resonance knob sets the amount of *delay feedback*, which is how many times the delay (or echo) will repeat before fading away. Finally, when the AM filter is selected, the Resonance knob becomes a Mix knob, where turning to the left will mix in more of the unfiltered sound coming from the Malström's oscillator(s), while turning it to the right will mix in more of the Ring Modulated signal.

■ **Mode (Filter Mode)**—Selects which type of filter will be active.

The Malström's two filters are quite different from most synthesizer filter sections. This is most apparent when considering the filter types that are available. While the inclusion of Low Pass and High Pass filters is pretty standard, the Comb filters and AM filters are intriguing and unique additions to the Malström's filter compliment. The Malström offers the following five filter types, selectable with the Mode button (see Figure 2.10).

Figure 2.10

The Malström's filters include some interesting filter types, including Comb filter and AM filter.

■ **LP 12**—The 12-Decibel Low Pass filter allows low frequencies to pass through, but filters high frequencies with a roll-off curve of 12 dB per octave. This is a very nice filter to sweep, especially with a bit of resonance.

■ **BP12**—The 12-Decibel Band Pass filter selects a band (or group of frequencies) to pass through, while filtering out (attenuating by 12 dB per octave) frequencies above and below that band. The specific frequency at which the Band Pass filter's affect is concentrated is determined by the value of the Freq (Cutoff Frequency) knob, while the size of the frequency band (or *bandwidth*) is determined by the value of the Resonance knob.

- ■ **Comb (+/–)**—The Comb filter creates a (very slightly) delayed version of its input signal and then adds that slightly delayed signal to the original input signal. This causes phase cancellations that result in a frequency response, which, when visually represented, shows a series of regularly occurring spikes like the teeth of a comb (thus the name). When using the Comb filter, the Resonance knob controls the amount of feedback (how many times the delay repeats before fading out), and high Resonance settings will result in higher, more sharply pronounced peaks in the frequency spectrum. The Freq knob controls the delay time. Turning the knob to the left results in longer delay times, while turning it to the right produces shorter delay times. This may seem counter-intuitive; however, turning it to the left produces lower resonant frequencies, while turning it to the right produces higher resonant frequencies. It is easy to hear differences in the delay times and the resonant frequencies with the Resonance knob turned all the way up (careful with your speakers/ears). The difference between Comb + and Comb– is in the position of their peaks relative to the overall frequency spectrum. In some cases, it is difficult to clearly discern an audible difference between the two, although higher Resonance settings with Comb– will usually result in quite a noticeable bass cut (attenuation of low frequencies).

- ■ **AM**—Ring Modulation is a form of Amplitude Modulation (AM), and this filter is actually a Ring Modulator (please see the explanation of Ring Modulation in Chapter 1). With the AM filter, the Resonance knob controls the mix between the input signal (from Osc A or Osc B) and the Ring Modulated signal (which consists of two frequencies, the sum and difference of the input signal and carrier signal). If you turn the Resonance knob all the way to the left, you will only hear the dry signal from the oscillator(s), and if you turn it all the way to the right, you will hear only the filtered (Ring Modulated) output. The Freq knob actually sets the frequency of the carrier signal (which is a sine wave). Sweeping the frequency of the carrier signal by turning the Freq knob while playing through the AM filter can create some pretty crazy sci-fi sounds. The frequency of the carrier signal can be further controlled according to which key you play if you have the kbd (Keyboard Tracking) button engaged.

You will have an opportunity to play with the AM filter during the exercise portion of the Filter Envelope discussion (which follows). But before moving on to the Filter Envelope, I would like you to get some hands-on experience with the Comb +/– filters.

1. Create an instance of the Malström. The Initialization Patch will be loaded by default.

2. By default, the Oscillator A Graintable Selector window should display Sine. Click the Graintable Selector Up arrow a few times to select Sawtooth. (The full name would be Wave: Sawtooth.) I have chosen Sawtooth because it is a simple, naked waveform, and also because it is, in a sense, the most "complete" waveform. As you read in Chapter 1, "The Subtractor," the Sawtooth wave contains all the audible harmonics. Turn your speakers or headphones down a bit for the sake of safety. Play a few notes to hear what the unadulterated Sawtooth wave sounds like.

3. Click the Route Oscillator A to Shaper button at the far right of Oscillator A (see Figure 2.11). It should light up. You will not actually be using the Shaper here (it will remain disengaged), but the signal must flow through the Shaper (bypassing the actual Shaper effect, which is turned off by default) on its way to Filter A. Play a few keys, and you will notice that much of the high-frequency content of the Sawtooth wave has been filtered out. This is because, by default, Filter A is already active and set for the 12-db Low Pass filter (which allows low frequencies to pass unimpeded, but filters out high frequencies). By default, the Filter A Freq knob is set at 12 o'clock, so it is filtering out about half the high frequencies it is capable of filtering.

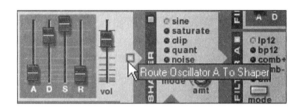

Figure 2.11

Engaging the Route Oscillator A to Shaper button is necessary for the signal to flow to Filter A, but the signal will bypass the Shaper effect if the Shaper itself is not engaged.

4. Turn the Filter A Resonance knob to 9 o'clock (a value of 25) and turn the Filter A Freq knob all the way to the right. Since you are using the 12-dB Low Pass filter (for the moment), the Resonance knob has the effect of emphasizing the frequency selected with the Filter A Freq knob.

5. Use the Filter A Mode button to select Comb+. Now the Resonance knob is actually controlling the amount of delay feedback (how many times the almost inaudibly short Comb filter echo repeats). The Freq knob is now controlling the delay time (the duration of an individual echo) of the Comb filter.

6. Hold down a note or chord while slowly dragging the Filter A Freq knob from right to left (all the way to the left). You should hear an effect known as *flanging*, which Wikipedia.org says "occurs when two identical signals are mixed together, but with one signal time-delayed by a small and gradually changing amount, usually smaller than 20 milliseconds." (I couldn't have said it better myself.) And hey, that's exactly what you just did! As you sweep the Freq knob to the far left, you may hear some variation in pitch. This is a side effect of changing the digital delay time while the signal is passing through the delay "circuit." Now let go of the note(s) you are holding and turn the Filter A Freq knob all the way to the right. Play a few notes just to reorient yourself in regard to the effect of the Comb+ filter.

7. Use the Filter A Mode button to select Comb— (see Figure 2.12). Now play a few notes. Notice that most of the bass has been filtered out. Hold down a note or two as you slowly turn the Filter A Freq knob all the way to the left (the shortest possible delay time).

8. Turn the Filter A Resonance knob all the way to the right. This is the maximum delay feedback setting (the maximum delay, echo, or number repeats). Play some keys, and you will hear undeniable proof of the Comb filter's use of delay. It should sound like you are playing inside of a large aluminum tube with reflections galore.

9. Hold down a note or two and slowly turn the Filter A Freq knob all the way to the right and back again and freak out to whatever extent satisfies you. You will hear that, indeed, sweeping the delay time of the Comb filter does effectively sweep the resonant frequency. Also, it sounds freaking weird.

Figure 2.12

Use the Filter A Mode button to select Comb—.
Or, if you like, it is also possible to select Comb—
by clicking directly on the Comb— indicator light.

Filter Envelope

The Filter Envelope can be assigned to control either one or both of the Malström's filters. This assignment is done by engaging the Env (Envelope) button of Filter A or Filter B. The Filter Envelope should look comfortably familiar to you, since it is a standard ADSR (Attack, Sustain, Decay, Release) envelope just like the ones you will find all over Reason and on most synthesizers. For a detailed discussion of ADSR, please refer to Chapter 1 and review the section entitled "ADSR: Four Letters You Cannot Live Without."

In addition to the ADSR sliders, there is an Amount knob, which controls the degree to which the Filter Envelope will affect the cutoff frequency of Filters A and B. There is also a Filter Envelope Invert button, which turns the whole Filter Envelope upside down. For instance, the Decay parameter would normally control how fast the cutoff frequency is lowered. With the Filter Envelope Invert button engaged, this is reversed, and the cutoff frequency of Filter A or B will increase by the same amount at the rate set by the Decay parameter.

Let's use the Filter Envelope to explore a couple of the Filter modes the Malström has to offer, starting with the Comb filter. In the following exercise, you will see how the Filter Envelope can be used in conjunction with the Comb— filter to create a formant sweep.

1. Create an instance of the Malström. The Initialization Patch will be loaded by default.

2. By default, the Oscillator A Graintable Selector window should display Sine. Click the Graintable Selector Up arrow a few times to select Sawtooth. (The full name would be Wave: Sawtooth.)

3. Click the Route Oscillator A to Shaper button at the far right of Oscillator A. It should light up.

4. The Filter A On/Off button should be on by default (see Figure 2.13). Turn the Filter A Resonance knob to 12 o'clock (a value of 64). You can leave the Filter A Freq knob at its default setting of 12 o'clock.

Filter A On/Off Button

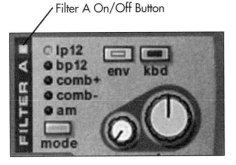

Figure 2.13

In a freshly initialized Maltröm, the Filter A On/Off button should be on by default.

5. Use the Filter A Mode button to select Comb–. By default, the Filter A Envelope button is engaged and lit up, signifying that the Filter A cutoff frequency is being modulated by the Filter Envelope. However, you will not hear any effect at this point because the Filter Envelope Amount knob is set to a zero value by default.

6. Set the Filter Envelope Amount knob to a value of 30 (just past 9 o'clock).

7. Set the Filter Envelope Decay slider to a value of 75. The other ADSR sliders can remain at their default values (Attack=0, Sustain=64, Release=10).

8. Play some keys in the lower register, and you will hear them each time the Filter Envelope is triggered; the formant (prevailing vowel sound) sweeps in a way that would be spelled something like AAAAAOOOOOUUUUU. As the Filter Envelope cycles through the Decay portion of its shape, the Filter A cutoff frequency is swept downward. Because you are using one of the Comb filters, this is actually decreasing the delay time of the Comb filter to achieve this effect.

9. At the moment, we are only using one oscillator, and the sound is mono (speaking in terms of the stereo image). Let's make it a little more fat. Turn on Oscillator B by clicking its power button in the upper-left corner of Osc B (the button should light up yellow). Click on the Oscillator B Graintable Selector window (so that you see the long vertical pop-up menu) and select Wave: PWM (which stands for Pulse Width Modulation).

10. Click the Route Oscillator B to Filter B button at the far right (bottom) of Oscillator B. It should light up yellow.

11. The Filter B On/Off button should be on by default. Set up Filter B so that its settings are identical to those of Filter A. Filter mode is Comb–, the Envelope button is engaged (lit up yellow), and the Resonance and Freq knobs should be set at 12 o'clock.

12. Turn the Spread knob (in the lower-left corner of the Malstrom) all the way to the right (its maximum value). Now the audio signal coming out of Filter A is panned all the way to the left of the stereo image, and the audio signal from Filter B is panned all the way to the right (see Figure 2.14).

Figure 2.14

Your Comb Envelope patch should look like this when you are done. The Filter Envelope is modulating the delay time of the Comb filter.

In case you would like to check your work in the preceding exercise, I have saved a version on your CD in the Malström Patches folder. The patch is named Comb Envelope.

In the next exercise, you will use the Filter Envelope in conjunction with the AM filter.

1. Create an instance of the Malström. The Initialization Patch will be loaded by default.

2. You can leave Oscillator A set to its default Sine Graintable for the moment.

3. Click the Route Oscillator A to Shaper button at the far right of Oscillator A. It should light up. Again, we are not using the Shaper effect, but the signal is routed through the Shaper section (bypassing the Shaper effect) on its way to Filter A.

4. The Filter A On/Off button should be on by default. Use the Filter A Mode button to select AM. Turn the Filter A Resonance knob all the way to the right (its maximum value). Remember that when using the AM filter (which is really a Ring Modulator), the Filter Resonance knob becomes a Mix knob, with the dry signal from the oscillator on the left, and the Ring Modulated signal on the right. You can leave the Filter A Freq knob at its default setting of 12 o'clock.

5. Play a few keys, and you will hear the effect of Ring Modulation (from the AM filter). At this point, the frequency of the Ring Modulator's input signal (coming from Oscillator A) is changing each time you play a different key, but the unheard *carrier signal* is remaining at a constant frequency. The set frequency of the carrier signal is determined by the Filter A Freq knob.

6. Click the Filter A Keyboard Track (Kbd) button. It should light up. Now the Filter A cutoff frequency (the frequency of the AM filter's carrier signal) will be modulated by the note value of whatever key you play. Play around on your keyboard to hear this effect. You will hear a more dramatic change in pitch from key to key than you did before engaging the Filter A Kbd button. In fact, at the default Cutoff Frequency setting of 64 (12 o'clock), the sidebands created by the Ring Modulator blend to produce the same perceived pitch as the input signal (but with more harmonic overtones). You will only hear a noticeable Ring

Modulator effect at this point if you turn the Filter A Freq knob to the right or left. After you are done experimenting with this, please return the Filter A Cutoff Frequency knob to its default value of 64 (12 o'clock).

7. By default, the Filter A Envelope button is engaged and lit up, signifying that the Filter A cutoff frequency is being modulated by the Filter Envelope. Please leave this button engaged. You will not hear any effect at this point, because the Filter Envelope Amount knob is set to a zero value by default.

8. Set the Filter Envelope so that Attack=79, Decay=100, Sustain=64, and Release=10. Then set the Filter Envelope Amount knob to a value of 44. Play a chord (preferably in the second octave above Middle C) and hold it for a few seconds. When I do this, I imagine Lynda Carter in her Wonder Woman costume jumping really high in slow motion. If you have never seen that TV show, you are encouraged to imagine whatever you like. Anyway, you can clearly hear the pitch rise during the Attack portion of the Filter Envelope, and then fall during the (slightly longer) Decay portion of the Filter Envelope (see Figure 2.15).

Figure 2.15

Your Wonder Woman patch should look like this when you are done. The Filter Envelope is being used to sweep the frequency of the AM filter's carrier signal (as originally set by the Filter A Cutoff Frequency knob).

In case you would like to check your work on the preceding exercise, I have saved a version on your CD in the the Malström Patches folder. The patch is named Wonder Woman.

Shaper

The Shaper, when activated, applies waveshaping synthesis to the incoming signal, thereby changing the shape of the incoming waveform. (But why do they call it the Shaper?) Here are descriptions of the different Shaper modes:

- **Sine**—This mode applies the smooth shape and sound of a Sine wave to the signal being routed through the Shaper.

- **Saturate**—This mode applies a warm, smooth distortion to the signal being routed through the Shaper.

■ **Clip**—When an audio circuit is fed a hotter signal than it is designed to handle, *clipping* occurs, which is a form of distortion. It is called clipping because, as the amplitude of the waveform (the height of the wave) exceeds the limits (or available headroom) of the audio circuit, the portion of the waveform that is beyond the capability of the audio circuit is simply cut off (or *clipped*). A clipped Sine wave, for instance, would "flatten out" at the top and bottom of the waveform as it hits the ceiling of the available headroom. This can sound sweet and warm when the clipping occurs in a vacuum tube circuit (as in a guitar amplifier) or when magnetic tape is pushed to its limit. However, digital distortion (like the Clip mode of the Shaper is designed to simulate) tends to be rather harsh and extreme. The Shaper's Clip mode does not sound so ridiculously nasty as digital distortion often does, though, and is really only a bit stronger than the effect of the Saturate mode.

■ **Quant**—Short for quantization, this Shaper mode can be used to produce bit-reduced sounds, such as the sound of old 8-bit drum machines (a standard audio CD is recorded at a quantization level of 16-bits). The term *quantization* in this sense does not refer to evenly aligning MIDI notes to a prescribed time division (as it does in the Reason Sequencer). Instead, quantization refers (in this case) to the method by which a continuous analog signal is converted into a non-continuous digital signal. Lower bit depths will result in lower fidelity sound with more audible artifacts. This would not be desirable in a piece of playback equipment (like a CD player), but it can be a cool color to introduce when designing synth sounds and creatively processing audio during production.

■ **Noise**—Although this mode is part of the Shaper, it is not exactly shaping the incoming waveform. Instead, it is multiplying the incoming waveform with noise.

Let's take a moment to try out the Shaper.

1. Create an instance of the Malström. The Initialization Patch will be loaded by default. Click on the Oscillator A Graintable Selector window (so that you see the long vertical pop-up menu) and select Perc: Tabla. Play a few notes to hear what this sounds like.

2. Turn off Filter A. Now click the Route Oscillator A to the Shaper button at the far right of Oscillator A. The button will light up.

3. Turn on the Shaper by clicking the button in the upper left of the Shaper. Sine is selected by default. The Reason manual says the following about the Shaper's Sine mode: "This produces a round, smooth sound." Turn the Shaper Amount knob all the way to the right and play your "Table." Does that sound round and smooth to you? Oh well.

4. Turn the Shaper Amount knob down to 12 o'clock. Now you have a more useful, processed percussion sound (see Figure 2.16).

5. The Tabla is a good sound to experiment with, as it's easy to hear the personality of the different Shaper modes. With the Shaper Amount knob at 12 o'clock, try all the Shaper modes one by one with the Tabla. Then try the same thing, but with the Shaper Amount knob all the way to the right (at maximum).

Figure 2.16

Shaper powers: Activate! Shape of . . . a Sine wave! Form of . . . a Tabla!

It's worth noting that if you care to, you can route the output of Filter B to the Shaper. At the top of Filter B (directly under the Shaper), there is a button inside an upward pointing arrow, which is the Route Filter B to Shaper button.

Modulator Section

The Malström has two modulators, each with something different to offer (see Figure 2.17). Both modulators are actually low-frequency oscillators (LFOs), which, as discussed in Chapter 1, oscillate at frequencies below the range of human hearing and are not used to produce sound. Instead, they are used to modulate (or change) various Malström parameters, according to the waveforms produced by the low-frequency oscillators. In addition to producing steadily repeating waveforms, each Malström modulator is also capable of producing a *1-Shot*, which means that the modulator only sweeps through the LFO's waveform one time (one cycle). This effectively creates an *envelope* in the shape of the specified waveform. Both modulators can be synced to the tempo of your Reason song if you wish, or their rates can be set independent of the song tempo. With the exception of the Modulator Rate control, all the knobs in the Modulator section are bipolar, which means they can have positive or negative values. By default, all the knobs are set at 12 o'clock (a value of zero), so they have no effect (except for the Rate knob). Turning any bipolar control knob to the right will result in a positive value, and turning it to the left will result in a negative value. The following parameters are common to both Modulator A and Modulator B.

Figure 2.17

The Modulator section of the Malström offers an incredible amount of control over your sound.

- **On/Off**—Turns the modulator on or off.

- **Curve**—Selects which waveform will be generated by the modulator's low-frequency oscillator (LFO). These modulators have some really cool waveforms! Scroll through them and check them out. The graphics are quite descriptive of what you can expect sonically.

- **1-Shot**—When the 1-Shot button is activated, the modulator will only cycle through its waveform once each time it is triggered, instead of continuing to cycle repeatedly.

- **Sync**—When Sync is engaged, the modulator will cycle in time with the song tempo. The Modulator Rate values will be expressed in musical time divisions (1/4, 1/8, and so on).

- **A/B Selector**—Routes the modulator signal to Oscillator A, Oscillator B, or both.

- **Rate**—Sets the speed at which the modulator will cycle through its waveform. In other words, it sets the frequency of the modulator's LFO. When Sync is off, this value will be expressed as a MIDI value between 0 and 127. When Sync is on, the Modulator Rate value will be expressed as a time division. If Show Parameter Value Tool Tip is selected on the General page of the Reason preferences, then you can check the Rate value by placing the cursor on top of the Rate knob with your mouse.

The following parameters are specific to Modulator A and are all bipolar:

- **Pitch**—Modulates the pitch of Osc A, Osc B, or both.

- **Index**—Modulates the index (the point at which the selected Graintable begins playing back) of Osc A, Osc B, or both.

- **Shift**—Modulates the shift (the size of the individual grains in the selected Graintable) of Osc A, Osc B, or both. Modulating the Shift parameter results in an adjustment in the harmonic character, or *formant*, of the overall sound.

The following parameters are specific to Modulator B and are all bipolar:

- **Motion**—Modulates the motion (the speed at which the oscillator sweeps through the selected Graintable) of Osc A, Osc B, or both.

- **Volume**—Modulates the volume level of Osc A, Osc B, or both.

- **Filter**—Modulates the cutoff frequency of Filter A, Filter B, or both.

- **Mod:A**—Allows Modulator B to change the total amount of modulation from Modulator A.

Each of the Malström's two modulators (LFOs) have 32 waveforms to choose from (which are referred to as *curves* within the Malström). They are not named, other than by number (Curve 1, Curve 2, and so on). The Curve number can only be seen if you mouse over the Curve Display window and you have the Show Parameter Value Tool Tip option checked on the General page of the Reason Preferences. Please take a moment to familiarize yourself with these curves.

1. Create an instance of the Malström. The Initialization Patch will be loaded by default, which includes a Sine wave Graintable for Oscillator A.

2. Turn the Modulator A Pitch knob up to 3 o'clock. The default curve is a Sine wave, which is numbered as Curve 0. Play a key on you MIDI keyboard to hear the familiar sound of the modulator's Sine wave modulating the pitch of Oscillator A.

3. Click the Curve Selector Up Arrow once to select Curve 1, which is a bipolar Triangle wave. Play the C4 key on your MIDI keyboard, and it will sound like you are about to eat some ghosts on Pac-Man.

4. One at a time, scroll up through the curves of Modulator A, stopping to play and listen to each one. There are some very interesting waveforms to choose from. Notice that some of the curves are unipolar (they start at the vertical midpoint and go up—you only see an upper half to the curve) while others fill up the entire Curve Display window.

5. To hear a good example of the difference between a unipolar curve and a bipolar curve, select Curve 25 (see Figure 2.18). To verify that you have selected Curve 25, you can mouse over the Curve Display window, and in a second, a Tool Tip will pop up that says Curve 25.

6. Turn off Modulator A by clicking the On/Off button in the upper-left corner. The yellow light should turn off. Now play a specific note on your keyboard. (I chose C4 again.) Now turn Modulator A back on. If Modulator A Pitch is still turned up to 3 o'clock, you should be able to play that same note and hear the original pitch alternating with incrementally descending pitches.

7. Now use the Modulator A Curve Selector Up arrow to select Curve 26 (see Figure 2.18). This is a bipolar version of the same curve. Play the same note on your keyboard again, and this time you will hear alternating incrementally descending notes above *and below* the original pitch.

Figure 2.18

Curve 25 and Curve 26 are two versions of the same waveform. The difference is, Curve 25 is unipolar, and Curve 26 is bipolar.

For the sake of clarity and simplicity, I asked you to simply modulate the pitch of one oscillator with these waveforms. But you can modulate so much more, and with so many routing options. Next, we are going to use the 1-Shot feature of the modulator to create an extra envelope.

1. Create an instance of the Malström. Set Oscillator A Graintable to Voice: BreathVoices. Set the Oscillator A Amp Envelope so that Attack=64, Decay=100, Sustain=127, and Release=71. Play a chord to hear what this sounds like.

2. Turn on the Route Oscillator A to Shaper button at the far right of Oscillator A. Play a chord to hear what this sounds like.

3. Leave Filter A set with its defaults, then set the Filter Envelope so that Attack=91, Decay=100, Sustain=0, Release=82, and Envelope Amount=74. Hold another chord to hear the shape of the Filter Envelope. It should be somewhat reminiscent of the ocean (but pitched). Turn off Oscillator A for the moment.

4. Turn on Oscillator B and select the Voice: MaleChoir Graintable. Set the Oscillator B Amp Envelope so that Attack=64, Decay=100, Sustain=127, and Release=71. Play a chord to hear what this sounds like.

5. Click the Route Oscillator B to Filter B button at the lower right of Oscillator B.

6. Set the Filter B Mode to BP 12. Leave the Cutoff Frequency at 12 o'clock and set the Resonance at 41. Turn off the Envelope button.

7. On Modulator B, turn on the 1-Shot button and choose Curve 20 (Unipolar Sine wave, looks like a frown). Set the Rate knob to 9 o'clock and the Filter knob to 3 o'clock. Set the A/B switch on the far right to its downward position so the Modulator B only modulates Filter B.

8. Turn Oscillator A back on.

9. In the lower right of the Malstrom, set the Volume to 85 and the Spread Amount to 40. Hold some chords, and you will hear the two similar but slightly different envelopes slowly opening and closing, with BreathVoices through Filter A (being controlled by the Filter Envelope) on the left, and MaleChoir through Filter B (being controlled by Modulator B) on the right (see Figure 2.19).

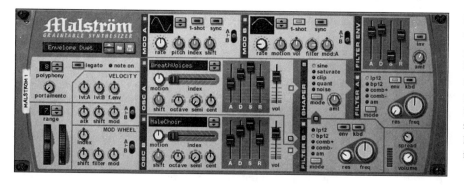

Figure 2.19

Your Envelope Duet patch should look like this when you are done. In this patch, Modulator B is being used as a second Filter Envelope, thanks to its 1-Shot feature.

In case you want to check your work on the previous patch, I have saved it on your CD in the Malström Patches folder with the name Envelope Duet.

Now I am going to teach you how to build an elegantly minimal, pretty, and yet somewhat advanced patch using both modulators, plus a bit of CV routing. I hope you like this one as much as I do.

1. Create an instance of the Malström. The Initialization Patch will be loaded by default, which includes a Sine wave Graintable for Oscillator A. My favorite!

2. Set Oscillator A Release to 60.

3. Select Curve 24 for Modulator A. Click the Modulator A Sync button to turn it on. (It should light up.)

4. Turn the Modulator A Rate knob to a time division value of 1/4. Then switch the Modulator A Target A/B switch (at the far right) to the Up position so that Modulator A will modulate Oscillator A only.

5. Set the Modulator A Shift knob to 3 o'clock (a value of 40). Play a few notes to hear how this sounds.

6. Click the Oscillator B On/Off button so that it lights up. Osc B is also playing a Sine wave Graintable, which is fine. Set Oscillator B Release to 60.

7. Select Curve 23 for Modulator B. Click the Modulator B Sync button to turn it on. (It should light up.) Then set the Modulator B Rate knob to a time division value of 1/4.

8. Switch the Modulator B Target A/B switch (at the far right) to the Down position so that Modulator B will modulate Oscillator B only.

9. Unfortunately, Modulator B does not have a Shift knob, but that will not stop you from independently modulating the shift of Oscillator B. Press the Tab key on your computer keyboard to flip the Reason rack around.

10. By clicking and dragging, connect a virtual cable between Mod B Output and Shift Modulation Input (see Figure 2.20). Turn the Shift Modulation Input Trim Pot (the knob directly to the right of the Shift Modulation Input) up to 3 o'clock (a value of 105) and set the Shift Target A/B Switch to its lower (Oscillator B only) position.

11. Press the Tab key on your computer keyboard to flip the Reason rack around to face the front.

12. In the lower-right corner of the Malström, turn the Spread knob all the way to the right. Now play some chords and hear what you've got. If you like, you can save the patch by clicking the diskette icon to the right of the Malström's Patch Browser (see Figure 2.21).

In case you want to check your work, I have saved this patch on your CD in the Malström Patches folder under the name Stereo Steps. I have also created a simple Reason song by the same name in the Malström In Action folder so you can hear this patch synced up against a click. By the way, if you check my sequence in the Reason song, you will find that all I am doing is changing the chord I am playing once every four bars. The Malström modulators are doing the rest!

Remember that the rear-panel CV routing is not saved with the patch, so whenever you load this patch, you must then connect a virtual cable between Mod B Output and Shift Modulation Input on the rear of the Malström.

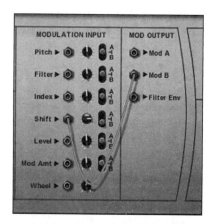

Figure 2.20

By clicking and dragging, connect a virtual cable between Mod B Output and Shift Modulation Input. Notice the modulation inputs each have a voltage trim potentiometer (or "pot," for short) that is used to attenuate or boost an incoming voltage by turning the knob to the left or right.

Figure 2.21

Your Stereo Steps patch should look like this when you are done. Using both modulators to independently control the Shift values of Oscillators A and B in distinct steps creates a surprising level of complexity in an otherwise delightfully minimal-sounding patch.

COMBINE YOUR PATCH

As I have just stated, rear panel CV routing is not saved with the Malström patch. There is a way around this problem (other than relying on your brain to always remember to correctly wire the rear panel after loading a patch). You can *combine* the Malström. This means you will save an additional Combinator patch, which will really be the complete patch, because it will include the rear panel routing. All you have to do is select the Malström by clicking once anywhere on it. Then, from your Edit menu, select Combine. Alternatively, you can right-click on the Malström (Ctrl-click, Mac) and select Combine from the pop-up menu that appears (see Figure 2.22). Now your Malström is inside of a Combinator. All you have left to do is click the little diskette icon to the right of the Combinator Patch Browser window and save the Combinator patch. The next time you recall it, a Combinator will launch, containing your the Malström, complete with its rear panel routing (see Figure 2.23).

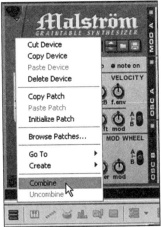

Figure 2.22

Combine the Malström, either by clicking on the Malström and selecting Combine from your Edit menu, or by right-clicking on the Malström (Ctrl-click, Mac) and selecting Combine from the pop-up menu that appears.

Figure 2.23

The Malström is now combined. Saving your patch as a Combinator patch ensures that any audio or CV routing you have done on the rear panel of the Malström will remain intact the next time you recall the Combinator patch.

Signal Flow in the Malström

Audio signal flow in the Malström is both flexible and intuitive. If you look at the Oscillator and Filter sections of the Malström, you will notice arrows indicating the direction of signal flow (see Figure 2.24). The basic path that the audio signal follows starts at the Oscillator section, flows through the Filter section (including the Shaper), through the Stereo Spread and Volume controls, and then out through the main audio outputs on the rear of the Malström (see Figure 2.25).

The Volume knob is the master output level control for the Malström. The Spread knob controls the relationship between the outputs of Filter A and Filter B in the stereo image. By default, the Spread knob is turned all the way to the left, which means that there is no stereo spread between Filter A and Filter B outputs. They both appear in the center of the stereo image, so the output of the Malström is mono. The farther to the right you turn the Spread knob, the farther apart these two signals diverge in the stereo image. The output of Filter A is panned farther and farther to the left, while at the same time the output of Filter B is panned equally farther and farther right in the stereo image. When the Spread knob is turned all the way to the right, the output of Filter A will be panned all the way to the left (you will only hear it in your left speaker), and the output of Filter B will be panned all the way to the right.

There is an exception to this description. Although by default, the output of Filter B does go through the Spread and Volume controls and then out the Main output, if you route the output of Filter B through the Shaper, it will flow out of the Shaper, then through Filter A, and eventually out the left Main output. In this scenario, it is not desirable to use the Spread feature, since this will result in no signal being routed through the right Main output. Note that although a signal may flow through the Filter B input (for instance) and then out through the Filter B output, the signal will bypass (or go around) the actual filter itself, unless two conditions have been met. First, the Filter B On/Off button must be on (lit); and second, the appropriate Route Oscillator to Filter B button must be lit up as well. These basic guidelines also apply to signals passing through the Shaper and Filter A.

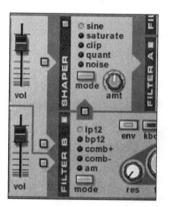

Figure 2.24

Look closely at the front of the Malström, and you will notice arrows indicating the audio signal path from Osc A to the Shaper and Filter B, from Osc B to Filter B, from Filter B up to the Shaper, and from the Shaper to Filter A. Both filters then feed into the Spread and Volume controls (though there are no arrows to indicate this).

Figure 2.25

The Main audio outputs on the rear of the Malström.

Velocity Routing

The Malström offers a variety of velocity routing options. Each knob in the Velocity section allows you to route velocity information to control the parameter for which the knob is named. All the Velocity controls are bipolar, so when a given Velocity control is set at its mid-point (12 o'clock) there will be no effect, while settings left of center will have an inverse effect on the selected parameter (higher velocities will affect the selected parameters negatively), and settings to the right of center will result in a positive effect on the selected parameter (higher velocities will affect the selected parameters positively).The following parameters can be controlled according to how hard you strike the keys on your keyboard (see Figure 2.26).

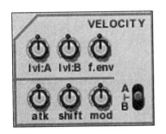

Figure 2.26

The Malström's Velocity routing section allows several parameters to be controlled according to how hard you strike the keys on your keyboard.

- **Lvl:A**—Controls the volume level of Oscillator A.
- **Lvl:B**—Controls the volume level of Oscillator B.
- **F.env**—Controls the Filter Envelope Amount.
- **Atk**—Controls the Attack time of either Oscillator A or Oscillator B, or both, depending on the position of the Velocity Target A/B switch.
- **Shift**—Controls the Shift of either Oscillator A or Oscillator B, or both, depending on the position of the Velocity Target A/B switch.
- **Mod**—Allows Velocity to simultaneously control all modulation amounts of either Modulator A or Modulator B, or both, depending on the position of the Velocity Target A/B switch.

Mod Wheel Routing

Like the Velocity controls, the Mod Wheel controls are bipolar; so settings left of center will have an inverse effect on the selected parameter (higher Mod Wheel values will affect the selected parameters negatively), and settings to the right of center will result in a positive effect on the selected parameter (higher Mod Wheel values will affect the selected parameters positively). Any Modulation Wheel controls set at 12 o'clock will have no effect. The following parameters can be controlled by the Modulation Wheel (see Figure 2.27).

Figure 2.27

The Malström's Modulation Wheel can be used to control Oscillator A and B Index and Shift, Filter A and B Cutoff Frequency, and Modulator A and B Modulation Amount.

- **Index**—Sets the positive or negative degree to which the Mod Wheel will control the currently active Graintable's Index parameter for Oscillator A or Oscillator B.

- **Shift**—Sets the positive or negative degree to which the Mod Wheel will control the Shift of either Oscillator A or Oscillator B, or both, depending on the position of the Mod Wheel Target A/B switch.

- **Filter**—Sets the positive or negative degree to which the Mod Wheel will control the Attack of either Oscillator A or Oscillator B, or both, depending on the position of the Mod Wheel Target A/B switch

- **Mod**—Sets the positive or negative degree to which the Mod Wheel will modulate the selected parameters of either Modulator A or Modulator B, or both, depending on the position of the Mod Wheel Target A/B switch.

Additional Play Parameters

In addition to the Velocity routing and Mod Wheel routing, the Malström offers the following additional Play parameters:

- **Polyphony**—Determines how many notes you can play at one time, selectable anywhere between 1 and 16 notes (see Figure 2.28). The Polyphony setting has no effect if the Legato button is engaged. Also, note that setting the polyphony to 1 (monophonic) does not allow the "pivot" action that you would get if you were using the Subtractor with a Polyphony setting of 1 (regardless of the Subtractor's Legato/ReTrig setting). Normally, on a monophonic synth, if you keep holding down one key while you hit a second key over and over again, each time you let go of the second key, you will again hear the first key that you are still holding down. This is not necessarily so with the Malström. To achieve this effect with the Malström, you must engage the Legato button.

- **Legato**—Legato works in a unique way on the Malström (see Figure 2.29). Instead of merely preventing the Filter Envelope from retriggering as long as you are holding down another note, the Malström's Legato function actually keeps the Graintable from retriggering. This effectively renders the Malström monophonic, regardless of the Polyphony setting. It also allows the nifty "pivot," or hammer-on technique, mentioned in the preceding Polyphony entry.

- **Portamento**—Determines the amount of time it takes to "glide" in pitch from one note to the next (see Figure 2.30). There is a bit more discussion regarding Portamento in the "Play Parameters" section of Chapter 1.

- **Pitch Bend**—The Pitch Bend wheel on the Malström (located directly to the left of the Modulation wheel) corresponds to the Pitch Bend on your MIDI keyboard, or it can be controlled with your mouse or with automation in the Reason Sequencer. Above the Pitch Bend wheel is the Pitch Bend Range control, with which you can select a Bend range of up to +/−24 steps, which is equal to two octaves (see Figure 2.31).

Figure 2.28

The Polyphony setting determines how many notes you can play at one time, selectable anywhere between 1 and 16 notes. The Polyphony setting has no effect if the Legato button is engaged.

Figure 2.29

Engaging the Legato button effectively renders the Malström monophonic, allowing only one note to sound at a time.

Figure 2.30

The Portamento setting determines the amount of time it takes to "glide" in pitch from one note to the next.

Figure 2.31

With the Malström's Pitch Bend wheel (and associated Range control), you can bend notes up or down by a degree of up to two octaves.

CV Routing

What follows is a description of the available control voltage inputs and outputs on the rear panel of the Malström. For additional information on control voltage, please refer to the "Control Voltage Routing" section in Chapter 1. Also, you will get into some hands-on CV routing in Chapter 5, "The Combinator," since the Combinator affords the opportunity to use several different Reason devices in conjunction with one another, with plenty of CV routing in between them. The Malström has the following control voltage inputs and outputs (see Figure 2.32).

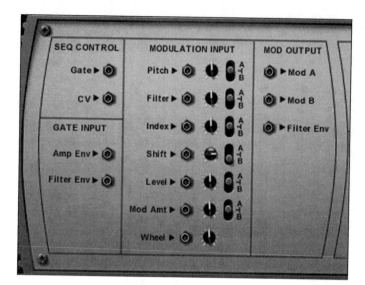

Figure 2.32

The Malström has extensive control voltage routing options.

- **Sequencer Control: Gate**—This input can receive Note On/Off and Velocity CV signals from another CV/Gate device (such as Matrix or ReDrum). This input is designed to receive monophonic information.

- **Sequencer Control: CV**—This input can receive Note Pitch CV signals from another CV/Gate device (such as Matrix or ReDrum). This input is designed to receive monophonic information.

- **Gate Input: Amp Envelope**—This input can receive control voltage from an external modulation source to trigger the Amp Envelopes of Oscillator A and B simultaneously. Note that with this input connected, you will no longer be able to trigger the oscillators by playing keys on your keyboard, as the Amp Envelope will only be controlled by the external modulation control voltage. However, each time the external modulation control voltage triggers the Amp Envelope, you will only hear the notes that you are holding down on the keyboard.

- **Gate Input: Filter Envelope**—This input can receive control voltage from an external modulation source to trigger the Malström's Filter Envelope. Note that with this input connected, you will no longer be able to trigger the Filter Envelope by playing keys on your keyboard, as the Filter Envelope will only be controlled by the external modulation control voltage. However, each time the external modulation control voltage triggers the Filter Envelope, you will only hear the Filter Envelope trigger for the notes that you are holding down on the keyboard.

- **Modulation Input**—These inputs each have a voltage *trim* potentiometer (or pot, for short). A *trim pot* is used to attenuate or boost an incoming voltage, in this case increasing or reducing the level of incoming modulation control voltage (with values left of center decreasing the voltage, and those right of center increasing the voltage). Each of the Modulation inputs also has an A/B switch, which allows each input signal to be routed to (Oscillator, Filter, Modulator) A, B, or both. The Malström has Modulation inputs for (Oscillator) Pitch, Filter (Cutoff Frequency), Index, Shift, (Oscillator volume) Level, Mod Amount (affects all front panel Modulation section levels simultaneously, depending on position of A/B switch), and (Mod) Wheel (for remote CV control of the Malström's Modulation wheel).

- **Mod Output: Mod A**—Sends control voltage from Modulator A to an external device or to a CV input on the Malström.

- **Mod Output: Mod B**—Sends control voltage from Modulator B to an external device or to a CV input on the Malström.

- **Mod Output: Filter Env**—Sends control voltage from the Filter Envelope to an external device or to a CV input on the Malström.

Audio Routing

In addition to a standard stereo output pair, the Malström has a couple of other interesting rear panel audio routing features (see Figure 2.33). It also has separate direct audio outputs for each of its two oscillators, and it even has an audio input, which allows the Malström to process an external audio signal through its filters and Shaper. Here is a description of the Malström's rear panel audio connections.

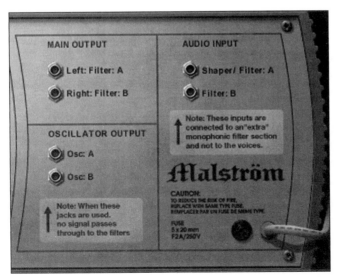

Figure 2.33

The rear panel audio connections provide another degree of flexibility for sound design with the Malström.

- **Main Output**—When the front panel Spread knob is turned all the way to the right (at its maximum value), the Left channel of the Main audio output comes entirely from Shaper/Filter A, and the right channel of the Main audio output comes from the output of Filter B. The distance between these two signals in the stereo image is determined by the front panel Spread knob. The farther to the left you turn the Spread knob, the more these two signals are mixed together. When the Spread knob is all the way to the left, the actual signal coming out of the left and right Main outputs is identical, resulting in a mono image.

- **Oscillator Output A and B**—These outputs allow you to route the signal coming directly from Osc A and B to an external device or to the audio inputs of the Malström. Note that connecting these outputs will interrupt the normal signal path of the Malström, so the Oscillator output will never be processed by the filters or the Shaper. However, you could route them to the monophonic version of the Shaper and filters using virtual patch cables on the rear of the Malström. You could also insert effects (such as the Scream 4 Distortion Unit or the DDL-1 Digital Delay Line) in between the oscillator output and the rear panel filter inputs.

- **Audio Input**—The audio inputs allow you to route audio signals to the Shaper/Filter A and to Filter B. When signals are routed this way, the filters and the Shaper will be monophonic, and the entire audio signal (no matter how many simultaneous notes it contains) will be routed through a single filter or the Shaper.

When using the standard internal routing in the Malström, the filters (and the Shaper) are polyphonic. Each note is processed separately, independent of the other. It is as though a separate instance of the filter or the Shaper is being applied to each individual note. I will be focusing on the Shaper in this discussion of polyphonic versus monophonic signal processing. First, I would like to share just a little of my personal experience regarding this topic. My story starts way back in the 1980s....

I started playing rock electric guitar when I was a teenager. (Yes, friends, you have purchased a technical book written by a guitarist!) Anyone who has played guitar through an overdriven amplifier or through a distortion pedal finds out that fancy jazz chords do not sound so sweet and defined when you play them with a bunch of distortion. For the most part, only single notes and "power chords" that have only two or three notes (the root and a fourth or the root and a fifth and perhaps an octave) sound smooth. Almost any other interval sounds "messy." This is actually an example of a monophonic waveshaper. The distortion is being applied to the whole signal, not to each note independently. I always wondered (and still do) what it would sound like to have each string amplified separately through a different overdriven tube amplifier. Then I could enjoy the sweet sustain and distortion without all the mess when I tried to play complex chords.

The Malström's Shaper has a couple of modes (Saturate and Clip) that distort the signal in a way similar to an overdriven audio circuit. Normally, the Shaper (like Filter A and Filter B) is polyphonic; that is, it's applied to each note separately. So even if you play a Gm7 flat 5 with Saturate turned all the way up, all the notes will still ring out distinctly. However, when you use external routing on the rear of the Malström to feed an audio signal into the Shaper/Filter A input, this engages a monophonic version of the Shaper (and of Filter A). So any combination of notes you play will be fed as a single signal through the Shaper. The next exercise will demonstrate this.

Remember, any routing you do on the rear of the Malström will *not* be saved with the patch. So for this patch to work when you recall it later, you have to remember to make a connection on the back of the Malström after loading the patch. By the way, the next time someone says that the synths in Reason sound thin, you don't have to resort to a 3-foot-high mega-Combinator patch to prove them wrong. This simple Malström patch should do the trick. I think this sounds best between Do and D3.

1. Create an instance of the Malström. The Initialization Patch will be loaded by default.

2. Change Oscillator A's waveform to Wave: Sawtooth*4, then click the little button on the far right of Oscillator A, which is the Route Oscillator A to Shaper button. It should light up.

3. Turn Filter A Freq to 87. Play a few notes and some chords to hear how this sounds.

4. Click the Shaper's power button so it lights up, set the Shaper Mode to Saturate, and turn the Shaper Amount knob all the way up. Play some more notes and chords, and the tone should sound a bit more fuzzy, distorted, or saturated. Still, even in a complex chord, each note should sound distinct.

5. Now flip your Reason rack around (by pressing the Tab key on your computer keyboard). Click and drag to draw a cable connecting Oscillator Output A to Audio Input Shaper/Filter: A (see Figure 2.34). Then flip the rack back around, and play some more chords. It should sound like you are playing through a guitar amp that is about to melt. Now is a good time to experiment with switching back and forth between the Clip, Quantize, and Saturate filter modes to hear the differences between them. When you are done experimenting, please make sure you are back in Saturate mode.

6. Turn on the Oscillator B On/Off button (so it lights up) and choose the Wave: Sawtooth*16 waveform.

7. Turn the Spread knob halfway up (see Figure 2.35). If you like the sound of this patch, you can save it by clicking the diskette icon to the right of the Malström's Patch Browser. Also, if you would like to check your work, this patch is already saved on your CD in the Malström Patches folder under the name Saturated Fat.

Now that you have used a virtual patch cable to connect the output of Osc A to the Shaper/Filter A audio input, it is no longer necessary to have the Route Oscillator A to Shaper button engaged. The rear panel routing supersedes the front panel routing, so if you disengage the Route Oscillator A to Shaper button, you will hear no difference. Remember that any time you load this patch into a fresh Malström instance, you will have to connect a virtual patch cable between Oscillator Output A and Audio Input Shaper/Filter: A on the rear panel of the Malström. Of course, as previously mentioned, the way around this is to *combine* the Malström and save everything as a Combinator patch.

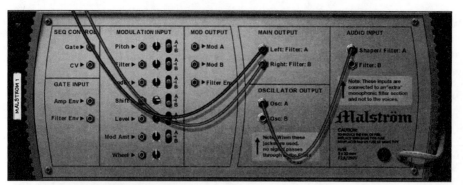

Figure 2.34

Click on Oscillator Output A and drag your mouse to connect a virtual patch cable to Audio Input Shaper/Filter: A.

Figure 2.35

Your Saturated Fat patch should look like this when you are done. The output of Oscillator A is being distorted by the "mono" version of the Shaper via rear panel audio routing.

3 NN-XT

The NN-XT Sampler is a truly advanced sample player (see Figure 3.1). While the NN-19 can do a comparatively limited range of operations with ease and speed, when it comes to depth of functionality, the NN-XT is definitely the deep end of the pool! It allows the creation of sample patches with multiple velocity layers for a new level of realism (when you play a note softly you hear one sample, when you play a little louder you hear another sample, and so on). Also included are eight stereo output pairs so that you can route individual zones to their own unique mixer channel, allowing you to process them individually with separate effects or EQ.

The NN-XT has a very professional feature set that allows you do pretty much anything you want with your samples. Although there is a level of complexity that comes along with such a wide range of powerful tools, you will find that the NN-XT actually includes several time-saving and easy-to-use features. Also, even though the big Remote Editor has a different graphical look and arrangement than what you have seen on other Reason devices, you will find a lot of familiar territory as soon as you begin working with it. If you have simply been using the NN-XT to load presets up until now, you are about to find out what you have been missing. It's like suddenly discovering that your car has a button on the dashboard that turns it into the Batmobile. Once you learn how to use the advanced features in the NN-XT Remote Editor, you will have a whole new level of control and creative power at your fingertips.

Figure 3.1

The NN-XT gives you all the control you need to develop great sample patches.

Main Panel

The Main Panel includes the Browse Patch button, which allows you to load NN-XT patches, as well as NN-19 patches, entire REX loops (the individual slices will be automatically mapped chromatically across the keyboard), and SoundFont presets. It also includes the Save Patch button for saving your custom sample patches. All the controls on the Main Panel of the NN-XT affect entire patches, instead of individual samples or key zones. Although only six knobs on the left of the Main Panel are actually labeled Global Controls, the other Main Panel controls are global as well. There are not many of them, so we can simply cruise through them from left to right (see Figure 3.2).

Figure 3.2

The Main Panel of the NN-XT.

- ■ **Pitch Bend Wheel**—The Pitch Bend wheel is used to raise or lower the pitch of the entire NN-XT patch (see Figure 3.2). It can be controlled with your mouse, with drawn-in Reason Sequencer automation, or with the Pitch Bend wheel on your MIDI keyboard. The Bend Range is set in the Remote Editor.

- ■ **Mod Wheel**—The Modulation wheel can be used to modulate a variety of parameters and can be controlled with your mouse, with drawn-in Reason Sequencer automation, or with the Mod wheel on your MIDI keyboard (see Figure 3.2). Which parameters should be modulated (and to what extent, positively or negatively) can be set in the Remote Editor.

■ **External Modulation Control**—If your MIDI keyboard has aftertouch, or an expression pedal jack, or if you have a MIDI breath controller, these MIDI messages can be used to control any of several parameters, determined by settings in the Remote Editor. Which sort of message is to be received (Aftertouch, Expression, or Breath) is determined by the Source button (see Figure 3.2). Unlike the other Reason Instruments, the NN-XT actually includes a separate External Modulation wheel, so that you can easily control the parameters to which External Modulation is routed with your mouse. This allows you to easily record Aftertouch, Expression, and Breath control messages into the Reason Sequencer, even if your MIDI controller does not have these features.

■ **Browse/Save Patch**—The familiar patch loading and saving apparatus, similar to the other Reason Instruments (see Figure 3.2). Includes up/down arrows to scroll through patches in the current folder (if any), a window displaying the currently selected patch, plus the familiar Browse Patch button (with the folder icon) and the Save Patch button (with the diskette icon).

■ **Note On Indicator**—Lights up whenever the NN-XT receives a MIDI Note On message (see Figure 3.2).

■ **High Quality Interpolation**—You will like the sound a lot better if you always leave this on, especially when you are dramatically repitching samples (see Figure 3.2). When activated, this setting requires a few extra CPU cycles in order to use a more complex interpolation algorithm for the calculation of sample pitch, resulting in higher fidelity, especially when repitching or using samples containing a lot of high frequencies. The impact on your CPU is negligible, but the impact on your sound can be somewhat severe if you forget to activate High Quality Interpolation!

■ **Filter Freq**—This is a bipolar control that positively or negatively offsets the Filter Frequency settings made in the Remote Editor (see Figure 3.2).

■ **Filter Res**—This is a bipolar control which positively or negatively offsets the Filter Resonance settings made in the Remote Editor (see Figure 3.2).

■ **Amp Envelope Attack**—When a note is played, the Amp Envelope Attack setting (see Figure 3.2) determines how long it takes for the sound to reach its maximum volume (amplitude). This is a bipolar control which positively or negatively offsets the Amp Envelope Attack settings made in the Remote Editor. Notice that this Global Amp Envelope section is a slightly simpler ADR envelope, as opposed to the ADSR envelopes we have seen so far. Sustain is left out of this global Amp Envelope. Not to worry—there is a new level of control waiting around the corner in the Amp and Filter Envelopes in the Remote Editor.

■ **Amp Envelope Decay**—When a note is played and held down, after the sound has reached its maximum amplitude (at a rate determined by the Amp Envelope Attack setting) and reached the end of its *hold duration* as set in the Remote Editor, the Amp Envelope Decay setting (see Figure 3.2) determines how long it takes for the sound to fall back down to the Sustain level set in the Remote Editor. This is a bipolar control which positively or negatively offsets the Amp Envelope Decay settings made in the Remote Editor.

- **Amp Envelope Release**—After a note has been played and released, the Amp Envelope Release setting determines how long it takes the note to fade away (see Figure 3.2). This is a bipolar control which positively or negatively offsets the Amp Envelope Release settings made in the Remote Editor.

- **Modulation Envelope Decay**—When a note is played and held down, after the sound has reached the end of the Attack and Hold portions of the Modulation Envelope in the Remote Editor, this bipolar control (see Figure 3.2) positively or negatively offsets the Modulation Envelope Decay settings made in the Remote Editor, influencing how long it takes the Modulation Envelope fall to the Sustain level set in the Remote Editor.

- **Master Volume**—Controls the overall volume level for the entire NN-XT patch (see Figure 3.2). I am pretty sure the little IR (Infrared Remote) window above the Master Volume control is just for looks. I pointed my universal remote at it, but nothing happened.

Remote Editor

Click the little arrow under the bottom left of the Main Panel to open the Remote Editor (see Figure 3.3). Now you can see where all the action is! The Remote Editor is the environment in which you will map samples across different velocity and key ranges, as well as adjust parameters for those individual samples. It offers a very high degree of control and has everything you need for intuitively creating expressive and original patches from your raw samples.

Figure 3.3

Clicking the little arrow under the bottom left of the Main Panel opens the Remote Editor, where all the magic happens!

Key Map Display

The big blue Key Map display is used not only to show information, but also to map key zones and velocity zones, audition samples, and select zones for editing (see Figure 3.4). The functions of the Key Map display are organized into the areas described in the following sections.

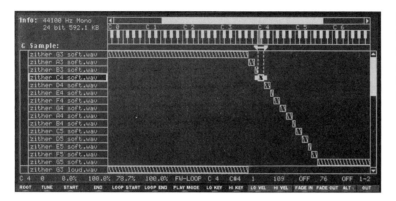

Figure 3.4

The Key Map display is used to show information, map key zones and velocity zones, audition samples, and select zones for editing.

Info Area

The Info area in the upper-left corner of the Key Map display shows the sample rate, bit depth, and file size of the sample contained in the currently selected zone. It also indicates whether the sample is mono or stereo (see Figure 3.5).

Figure 3.5

The Info area displays information about the sample contained in the currently selected zone.

Sample Area

The Sample area, located on the left side of the Key Map display, shows the names of the samples loaded into each zone. By clicking and dragging a sample up or down, you can change the order of the zones in the Key Map display (see Figure 3.6).

Figure 3.6

The Sample area displays the names of the samples loaded into each zone.

77

SAMPLES AND ZONES

The terms "sample" and "zone" will be used quite a bit in this section (as well as the rest of this chapter), and the use of these terms may seem confusingly synonymous at times. To clarify: A *sample* is an actual audio file that can be loaded into the NN-XT, and a *zone* is a virtual container for the sample. Making settings for a zone affects the playback of the sample it contains. Several zones can each contain the same sample, but if you set the parameters differently for each zone, that same sample will play back differently, depending on which zone is being triggered. Also, a zone could be completely empty, containing no sample at all.

Group Area

The Group area simply refers to the vertical rectangular area to the left of the Sample area. By clicking in the Group area, you can simultaneously select all the zones in a certain group (see Figure 3.7). By default, when multiple samples are loaded into the NN-XT, they are all part of the same group. In order to place some samples in their own group, Shift-click on the samples you want to group (they need not be sequential—other unselected samples can be in-between), and then select Group Selected Zones from the Edit menu (or from the Context menu that pops up when you right-click [Ctrl-click, Mac] on the NN-XT). Now, by clicking in the Group area, you will be able to select all the samples/zones in the group at once, and you will be able to drag the entire group up or down across the Key Map display.

Figure 3.7

Click in the Group area to simultaneously select all the zones in a certain group.

Keyboard Area

The Keyboard area is your visual reference for setting up key ranges (see Figure 3.8). Since not all available keys can fit on the display at the same time, you can use the horizontal scroll bar to see portions of the virtual keyboard that are to the right or left of the currently displayed portion. By Ctrl-clicking on a key, you can set the root key for the currently selected sample. By Alt-clicking on a key, you can audition the sample that is currently mapped to that key.

Figure 3.8

The Keyboard area is your visual reference for setting up key ranges.

Tab Bar Area

Just below the Keyboard area is the Tab Bar area, which displays the key range of the selected zone. You can resize a key range by clicking and dragging the boundary handles at either edge of the Tab Bar area (see Figure 3.9). If you click and drag the left boundary handle, you will see that low key value change above the Lo Key knob (below the Key Map display). Similarly, if you click and drag the right boundary handle, you will see the high key value change above the Hi Key knob (see Figure 3.10). To move an entire key range without changing its size, click on the area between the boundary handles and drag the key range to the right or left (see Figure 3.11). The root key will automatically be changed to correspond with the new location of the key range, unless you first engage the Lock Root Keys button above the upper left of the Key Map display, in which case the key range will still move, but the root key of the sample will stay the same.

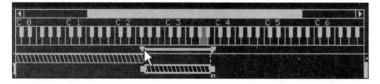

Figure 3.9

You can resize the key range of the currently selected zone by clicking and dragging the boundary handles at either edge of the Tab Bar area.

Figure 3.10

When you click and drag the left boundary handle of the Tab Bar area, you will see the low key value change, and when you click and drag the right boundary handle, the high key value will change.

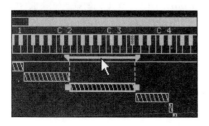

Figure 3.11

To move an entire key range without changing its size, click on the area between the boundary handles and drag the key range to the right or left.

Key Range Area

The Key Range area is located in the middle of the Key Map display and simultaneously shows all the zones (see Figure 3.12). You can move the zones in the Key Range area by clicking and dragging them, and you can resize them by clicking on their left and right boundary handles (see Figure 3.13), the same way you can with the Tab Bar area.

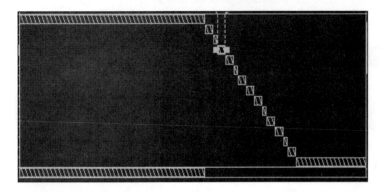

Figure 3.12

The Key Range area simultaneously displays all zones, which are selectable for editing, and can be moved and resized as well.

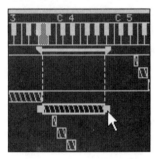

Figure 3.13

Just as in the Tab Bar area, you can move the zones in the Key Range area by clicking and dragging them, and you can resize them by clicking on their left and right boundary handles.

Scroll Bars

The Key Map display has vertical and horizontal scroll bars which can be used to show information that is currently off screen (see Figure 3.14). The entire range of available notes in the Keyboard area cannot fit on the Key Map display at one time, so you must use the horizontal scroll bar to see everything. Often all the zones in the Key Range area cannot be seen at one time, and you may have to use the vertical scroll bar to see the zone you are trying to select and edit. You can move the scroll bars either by clicking on the arrows at their edges or by clicking and dragging the scroll bar handles (the light-blue area in the center of each scroll bar). Note that the vertical scroll bar handle will only appear if there is more information than will fit vertically on one screen.

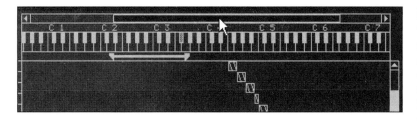

Figure 3.14

The vertical and horizontal scroll bars can be used to show information that is currently off screen. You can move the scroll bars either by clicking on the arrows at their edges or by clicking and dragging the scroll bar handles (pictured).

Using the Key Map Display/Edit Focus

The term Edit Focus may sound a little dry, but it is a simple and useful concept. Several zones can be selected at the same time for editing, but only one zone at a time may have Edit Focus (see Figure 3.15). This is important because, while the Synth, Group, and Multiple Adjustment Sample parameters will be applied to all currently selected zones (or currently selected groups of zones in the case of the Group parameters), the Single Adjustment Sample parameters only apply to the zone that has Edit Focus. So if you have several zones selected and adjust a Synth parameter such as Filter Resonance, the setting will be applied to all the selected zones, regardless of Edit Focus. But if you adjust one of the Single Adjustment Sample parameters (such as Root Key, Sample Start, or Loop End), the change will only be applied to the zone with Edit Focus, even if several other zones are also selected. You will read about these different types of parameters a little later in this chapter. As you do, you should keep the following points in mind regarding the selection of zones and Edit Focus.

Figure 3.15

Several zones can be selected at the same time for editing, but only one zone at a time may have Edit Focus. The Single Adjustment Sample parameters only apply to the zone that has Edit Focus.

- The zone with Edit Focus has a thicker outline and will have left and right boundary handles in the Key Range area (see Figure 3.16).

- When selecting zones, it does not matter whether you click on them in the Sample area or in the Key Range area.

- Clicking on a zone selects it and gives it Edit Focus.

81

■ Selecting a key zone via MIDI also gives the zone Edit Focus in addition to selecting it.

■ If several zones are selected at the same time (or a group of zones is selected), clicking on any of the already selected zones will give it Edit Focus, without deselecting the other zones.

■ Clicking in the Group area selects all the zones in that group but does not give any of them Edit Focus.

■ To select multiple zones (which can be non-contiguous), hold down the Shift key while clicking on the zone. To deselect a zone, hold down the Shift key and click on the zone you wish to deselect.

■ To select multiple contiguous zones, click and drag a selection box around the desired zones in the Key Range area (see Figure 3.17).

■ To select all zones, choose Select All Zones from the Edit menu or from the Context menu that pops up when you right-click (Ctrl-click, Mac) on the NN-XT. Alternatively, you can select all zones by pressing Ctrl+A (Command+A, Mac).

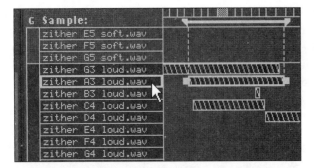

Figure 3.16

The zone with Edit Focus has a thicker outline and will have left and right boundary handles in the Key Range area.

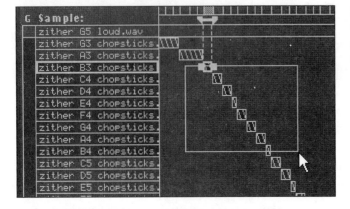

Figure 3.17

To select multiple contiguous zones, click and drag a selection box around the desired zones in the Key Range area.

There are three similar looking buttons above the Key Map display with radically different functions (see Figure 3.18).

Figure 3.18

Three similar buttons with three very different functions: Select Zone via MIDI, Solo Sample, and Lock Root Keys.

- **Select Zone via MIDI**—When this feature is activated, playing keys on your MIDI keyboard will automatically select the key zone in which those keys are included. This is an especially useful feature when tuning samples by ear or setting the volume levels of individual samples. This feature is velocity-sensitive, so if (for example) you have a zone mapped with a velocity range of 100 to 127, then you will have to hit a key within that zone sufficiently hard (at least with a velocity of 100) in order to use Select Zone via MIDI. Note that this feature is always turned off any time a new patch is loaded into the NN-XT, and it is off by default when the NN-XT is initialized. It cannot be saved with a patch.

- **Solo Sample**—The Solo Sample button allows the currently selected sample to be played over the entire keyboard instead of being restricted to its key zone. Any existing velocity ranges will be disregarded. In order for Solo Sample to work, you must select only one zone, or if multiple zones are selected, the sample you want to hear must have Edit Focus. Then you can activate the Solo Sample button. The Solo Sample feature will have no effect if Select Zone via MIDI is active.

- **Lock Root Keys**—Normally, when you move zones by clicking and dragging the entire zone in the Key Range area, or in the Tab Bar area, the root key of the zone(s) you are moving will change according to where you move the zone, thus causing the zone to be transposed. However, if you do not want the zone to be transposed, click the Lock Root Keys function before you move the zone(s). This can result in interesting effects, allowing you to have your samples play back at pitches radically different than those at which the samples were originally recorded, which will result in a completely different timbre and character to the sound.

Edit Menu/Context Menu Selections

The following selections can be made either from the Edit menu or the Context menu, which is the menu that pops up when you right-click (Ctrl-click, Mac) on the NN-XT.

- **Remove Samples**—Deletes the samples loaded into the currently selected zones.

- **Reload Samples**—Reloads the sample in each currently selected zone and undoes any changes you have made to the Single Adjustment Sample parameters (such as Root Key or Tune).

- **Add Zones**—Selecting this adds one empty zone.

- **Copy/Paste/Delete Zones**—Use these functions with zones the same way you would copy, paste, and delete in any other program.

- **Duplicate Zones**—Creates an identical copy of each currently selected zone.

- **Copy Parameters to Selected Zones**—This function is used to copy Synth parameter settings from one zone to one or more other zones. To do this, select the zone with the Synth parameters you wish to copy, and at the same time also select the zone(s) to which you would like to copy those parameters. Make sure to click on the zone with the parameters you want to copy to give it Edit Focus. Then select Copy Parameters to Selected Zones from the Edit menu (or from the Context menu). Now all the selected zones will have the exact same Synth parameter settings.

- **Sort Zones by Note**—Automatically sorts all selected zones within a group according to their key ranges.

- **Sort Zones by Velocity**—Automatically sorts all selected zones within a group according to their velocity ranges.

- **Group Selected Zones**—Groups all the currently selected zones, even if they are non-contiguous.

- **Set Root Notes from Pitch Detection**—Automatically sets root keys for the currently selected zones according to their pitch. Also, the samples will be automatically tuned to whatever extent is necessary to bring them to standard pitch. In order for Set Root Notes from Pitch Detection to work properly, the samples must have a discernable pitch. The NN-XT will have a much easier time correctly detecting the pitch of a sampled piano key than of a sampled thunderclap, for instance.

- **Automap Zones**—Automatically maps the currently selected zones according to their root keys. In order for this to work correctly, root key information must already be included in the sample files, or else the root keys must be set manually or set using Set Root Notes from Pitch Detection prior to clicking Automap Zones.

- **Create Velocity Crossfades**—If more than one zone is selected, each with different and partially overlapping velocity ranges, the Create Velocity Crossfades feature can automatically apply crossfades between the zones. This can be used to smooth the transition between one velocity range and the next. Note that velocity crossfades can be created manually using the Fade In and Fade Out knobs under the lower-left portion of the Key Map display.

Set Root Notes from Pitch Detection: A Closer Look

What a handy feature this is! If you have already gone through the NN-19 chapter (included as a PDF file on your CD-ROM), you will remember how when you were loading samples into the NN-19, you could only use the Automap Samples feature if there had already been root key information saved in the sample file. Otherwise, you had to set the root keys manually, one at a time. While most commercially available instrument samples will have root key information saved in the Wave or AIFF files, it is likely that any samples you make at home will not. Most people reading this book probably already own some software that can be used for recording and editing Wave or AIFF files. Pro Tools, Cubase, Sonar, Live, or any other DAW (Digital Audio Workstation) application will be able to do this. However, you may not own a program like Wavelab, which can save root key information with the audio file. That's where Set Root Notes from Pitch Detection is so useful. Once you have loaded some samples into the NN-XT, you can use this feature to automatically set the root key for each sample based on the actual pitch of the sample. It will also automatically and instantly correct the pitch of the samples, if needed! Then you can use Automap Zones (similar to the NN-19's Automap Samples feature) and see those homemade samples mapped across the keyboard in fine fashion. Please give it a quick try to see how easy it is.

1. Start with an empty rack and create an instance of the NN-XT.

2. Open the NN-XT Remote Editor and click the button labeled Load Sample to open the Sample Browser.

3. On your CD-ROM, browse to NN-19 > NN-19 Samples > Raw Bowls and select the four Wave files therein. You will see that they have all been loaded and that each sample's key range spans from C1 to C6. Click on each zone in the Key Range area (or in the Sample area), and you will see that each sample's root key is set at C3 (the default value) and that the Tuning parameter for each sample is set for zero.

4. From the Edit menu, select Set Root Notes from Pitch Detection. Now when you click on each zone, you will see that not only has the proper root key been set for each sample, but that a tuning adjustment has been made to each sample so that it is in perfect pitch relative to A440. Remember, these are bowls from my kitchen and did not happen to be tuned to any standard pitch. I had done pitch correction in Wavelab on the samples in the Prepared Bowls folder, but the NN-XT did it for us instantly for these samples from the Raw Bowls folder!

5. Now that the root keys have been assigned for each sample, right-click (Ctrl-click, Mac) on the NN-XT and select Automap Zones from the Context menu. Now each zone has its own unique key range, with its root key in the middle of the key range (see Figure 3.19).

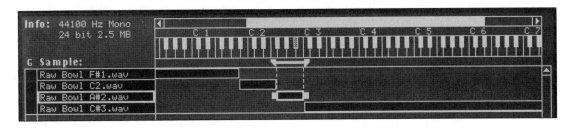

Figure 3.19

Thanks to Automap Zones, each zone now has its own unique key range, with its root key in the middle of the key range.

Sample Parameters

The Sample parameters refer to the knobs lining the bottom of the Key Map display (see Figure 3.20). The Sample parameters are divided into two groups, which are distinguished by different colors on the control panel. The knobs on the left against a darker gray background are the Single Adjustment parameters, and the knobs to the right are the Multiple Adjustment parameters. They are described in detail below.

Figure 3.20

Lining the bottom of the Key Map display are the Sample parameter knobs.
Their parameter values are displayed above the knobs at the bottom of the Key Map display.

Single Adjustment Parameters

The following parameters can only be adjusted for one zone at a time. Changes made to these parameters are only applied to the zone with Edit Focus (see Figure 3.21).

Figure 3.21

The Single Adjustment Sample parameters can only be adjusted for one zone at a time, and changes made to these parameters are only applied to the zone with Edit Focus.

- **Root**—Use this knob to manually set the root key for the zone with Edit Focus. Alternately, you can Ctrl-click on the appropriate key in the Keyboard area to manually set the root key.

- **Tune**—Use this knob to manually tune the zone with Edit Focus.

- **Sample Start/End**—These knobs are used to set the points in the sample at which playback will start and end for the zone with Edit Focus.

- **Loop Start/End**—Use these knobs to manually adjust the loop start point and loop end point of the zone with Edit Focus.

- **Play Mode**—Adjusts the loop mode for the zone with Edit Focus.

- **Lo Key/Hi Key**—Use these knobs to set the low key and high key for the key range of the zone with Edit Focus. As an alternative, you can click and drag the boundary edges of the zone in the Tab Bar area or the Key Range area.

Play Mode: A Closer Look

Play mode is similar to the NN-19's Loop Mode parameter but has a wider variety of choices (see Figure 3.21). The following Play modes are available for each zone.

- **FW**—Plays the sample forward once from start to finish without looping.

- **FW-Loop**—The most common Play mode, FW-Loop plays the sample forward once from the start of the sample to the loop end point, then back to the loop start point, continuing to cycle forward through the loop.

- **FW-BW**—Plays the sample forward once from the start of the sample to the loop end point, then from the loop end point to the loop start point, and backward and forward between the loop end and loop start points.

- **FW-SUS**—This setting functions in the same way as FW-Loop, except that it will only loop as long as a key is held down. When you let go of the key, the sample will play past the loop end point all the way to the absolute end of the sample. An effect of this is that even if you have a relatively long Amp Envelope Release setting, you will hear a short release when you let go of the key because the looping will not continue.

- **BW**—Plays the sample backward from finish to start once without looping. Makes including backward messages in your music easy. Seriously, it's cool to be able to make individual zones play backward!

AUDITIONING SAMPLES

Remember that as you apply Sample parameter adjustments to the individual zones, you can Alt-click (Option-click, Mac) on the zone to audition it and hear your changes. Your cursor will turn into a little speaker icon when you do this. If you Alt-click on a zone in the Sample area (see Figure 3.22), you will hear the effect of Sample parameters such as Loop End, but you will not hear the effect of any Synth parameters such as Pan, Amp level, or Filter settings. The sample will play at its root pitch. If you Alt-click a key on the virtual keyboard, you will hear any processing that has been applied to the sample (including any Synth parameters), and the sample will play back at the pitch corresponding to the key you clicked on the virtual keyboard, at a set velocity of 100. Alt-clicking on a key may actually trigger more than one sample, if indeed more than one sample has been mapped to that key with velocity ranges, including the value 100. Alt-clicking on a zone in the Key Range area does not audition the sample at all.

Figure 3.22

If you Alt-click on a zone in the Sample area, you will hear the effect of Sample parameters such as Loop End, but you will not hear the effect of any Synth parameters such as Pan, Amp level, or Filter settings.

87

Multiple Adjustment Parameters

To the right of the Single Adjustment Sample parameters are the Multiple Adjustment Sample parameters, which are visually distinguished by their gray background. The Multiple Adjustment Sample parameters described below can be applied to multiple selected zones simultaneously, regardless of Edit Focus (see Figure 3.23).

Figure 3.23

The Multiple Adjustment Sample parameters can be applied to multiple selected zones simultaneously, regardless of Edit Focus.

- **Lo/Hi Velocity**—By default, a newly loaded sample (and its zone) will have a full velocity range, with a low velocity of 1 and a high velocity of 127 (the minimum and maximum non-zero MIDI values). By setting the Lo Velocity knob, you can choose the lowest velocity at which a zone will be triggered. So if Lo Velocity is set for 64, and you hit a note more quietly at a velocity lower than 64, the zone will not trigger, and the note will not sound. The Hi Velocity control (when set below 127) means that any note sent at a higher velocity than the value of the Hi Velocity knob will not sound. These are the basic tools used for creating sample patches with multiple velocity layers.

- **Fade In/Fade Out**—These controls are used for manually creating velocity fades. An example would be if you have two zones triggered by the same note, one zone with a lower velocity range and one zone with a higher velocity range. Instead of having an abrupt change between samples when you hit a slightly higher or lower velocity, you can use these controls to have one zone gradually fade out as another gradually fades in, depending on how hard you strike the keys, thus achieving a more natural, less jarring effect.

- **Alternate**—This control, when activated, will cause multiple overlapping zones, to which it is applied semi-randomly, switch between each other each time the zones are triggered so that a different zone plays each time.

- **Out**—This control is used to assign the selected zones to any of the NN-XT's eight stereo output pairs.

Alternate: A Closer Look

The Alternate function can be used to semi-randomly alternate between overlapping zones during playback. Located at the bottom right of the Sample parameters section, the Alt knob has only two values—On and Off. When applied to a group of selected overlapping zones, the Alternate function switches between them using an algorithm designed to minimize repetition. This can be useful for adding realism to sequences. For instance, if a snare drum sample is mapped to a certain zone, you could create several more identical overlapping zones. If you had at your disposal several different samples of the same snare drum being hit, you could map a different snare sample to each overlapping zone, and then use the Alternate function to randomly switch between them each time that note is triggered. This would give a more realistic, human feel to the sequence. You could also apply this technique to samples of the bowing of stringed instruments, like violin or cello. The following exercise offers another application of the Alternate function and will give you a feel for how the feature operates.

1. Start with an empty rack and create instances of reMix, NN-XT, and Dr.Rex, in that order.

2. Click the NN-XT's Browse Patch button and load Reason Factory Sound Bank > Dr.Rex Drum Loops > Electronic > Elc34_Pioneers_110_eLAB.rx2. It's the last Rex loop in the Electronic folder.

3. Click Dr.Rex's Browse Patch button and load the same patch.

4. Select the NN-XT track in the Reason Sequencer. Then click the To Track button on Dr.Rex. You will receive a warning that you are about to write data to a track that controls an instrument other than the one selected. Click OK in the warning box. (We know what we're doing!) The MIDI data for the Rex loop will be written to the NN-XT Ssequencer track. Click Play on the Reason Transport Panel to hear the loop.

5. Open the NN-XT Remote Editor. Right-click (Ctrl-click, Mac) on the fifth sample in the Rex loop and select Duplicate Zones from the pop-up menu. Another identical zone will be created directly below the original.

6. Select Duplicate Zones from the Edit menu three more times so that you have five identical zones (see Figure 3.24). All the zones will have the same sample loaded. Alt-click in the Sample area on one of these identical zones to audition the sample.

7. If the loop is still playing, you will notice that having five identical overlapping zones causes that beat to be louder, since five instances of the same sample are playing simultaneously on each pass. While holding down the Shift key, click on all five zones so that they are highlighted, and then turn the Alternate knob to its On position (see Figure 3.25). You will notice the volume return to normal because now only one zone is being triggered at a time (chosen randomly by the Alternate algorithm).

8. Bring the second of the five identical zones into Edit Focus by clicking on it. Set the Play Mode knob to FW-Loop. Set the Loop End to 8.4%. Turn the Amp Envelope level down to −5 dB gain, and turn the Pan control to a value of −30, or about 10 o'clock.

9. Bring the third of the five identical zones into Edit Focus by clicking on it. Set the Play Mode knob to FW-Loop. Set the Loop End to 0.5%.

10. Bring the fourth of the five identical zones into Edit Focus by clicking on it. Set the Play Mode knob to BW. Turn the Amp Envelope level all the way up.

11. Bring the fifth of the five identical zones into Edit Focus by clicking on it. Set the Play Mode knob to FW-Loop. Set the Loop End to 22.2%. Turn the Amp Envelope level down to −5 dB gain, and set the Pan knob to a value of 30, or about 2 o'clock. If it is not already playing, click Play on the Reason Transport Panel and listen for a little while. You will hear the random fun you have injected into the mix.

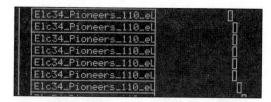

Figure 3.24

Select Duplicate Zones from the Edit menu three more times so that you have five identical zones.

Figure 3.25

While holding down the Shift key, click on all five zones so that they are highlighted, and then turn the Alt knob to its On position.

I have saved this exercise in the NNXT In Action folder with the name Alternate.

Velocity Ranges and Velocity Crossfades

Setting multiple zones with different velocity ranges to the same key range can add a whole new level of expressiveness and realism to your sample patches. Take a snare drum, for instance. If you had three recordings, one of a very soft snare hit, one medium snare hit, and one very hard snare hit, you could load all three of these into the NN-XT and assign all three zones to the same key range. You could turn the Pitch Keyboard Tracking knob all the way to the left so that pitch would not be affected by what key you play, allowing you to play the snare drum at the same pitch on more than one key. Then you could set the Lo and Hi Velocity controls for each of the three snare samples so that the soft snare sample would only be triggered by soft velocities, the medium snare sample would only be triggered by medium velocities, and the hard snare sample would only be triggered by very high velocities. You would then have a *multilayered sample patch*. If you wanted, you could set up velocity crossfades so that there would be smooth transitions between the three samples as you struck keys harder or more softly.

By default, any sample you load into the NN-XT will have a full velocity range of 1 to 127, so striking a key at any velocity will trigger the sample. As soon as you diminish this velocity range, either by turning up the Lo Velocity knob to a value greater than one or by turning down the Hi Velocity knob to a value less than 127, that zone will be shaded with diagonal lines to show that it has less than a full velocity range (see Figure 3.26).

The best way to get a feel for setting up velocity ranges and velocity crossfades is to actually do it for real. For the following exercise, I have prepared some samples. I used an inexpensive zither (see Figure 3.27), which can be purchased for under US$40. It is made in Belarus and sold in America with the product name Music Maker. It came with little paper inserts with which one could play songs such as "The Eensy-Weensy Spider" by following the dots on the page. It has 15 strings and is tuned to the C Major scale, spanning the notes G3 through G5. I sampled all 15

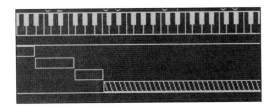

Figure 3.26

The bottom zone is shaded with diagonal lines to show that it has less than a full velocity range (the velocity range is less than 1 to 127).

strings three times. The first time, I plucked each string gently with my finger. The second time, I plucked each string as hard as I could with a guitar pick. The third time, I allowed a wooden chopstick to bounce on each string. Then I edited the samples in Wavelab. I also tuned the samples and assigned root keys to them in Wavelab, although the NN-XT could have done that part for me automatically with the Set Root Notes from Pitch Detection feature! I must enjoy extra work.

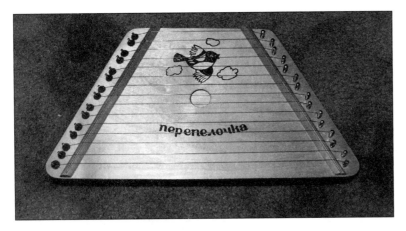

Figure 3.27

Thirty-seven dollars well spent! Each string on this little zither has been sampled with three different playing styles.

1. Start with an empty rack and add an instance of NN-XT. Click the arrow in the lower-left corner of the NN-XT to open the Remote Editor.

2. Click the Load Sample button in the upper left of the Remote Editor. On your CD-ROM, browse to NNXT > NNXT Samples > zither > zither soft. Select all 15 samples in the Zither Soft folder and click OK.

3. Click on an empty part of the Key Range area to deselect all the zones, and then click Load Sample again. This time, on your CD-ROM, browse to NNXT > NNXT Samples > zither > zither loud. Select all 15 samples in the Zither Loud folder and click OK.

4. All the samples you have just loaded from the Zither Loud folder should already be selected. The soft zither samples are not selected, but you can see by the darkened vertical Group area bar that both sets of samples are part of the same group (see Figure 3.28). From the Edit menu, select Group Selected Zones. Now the loud zither zones are all part of their own group, and the soft zither samples are part of another group (see Figure 3.29).

Figure 3.28

You can see by the darkened vertical Group area
bar that both sets of samples are part of the same group.

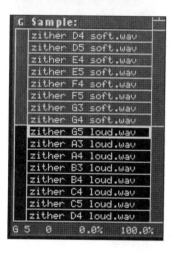

Figure 3.29

Now that you have applied Group Selected Zones,
the loud zither zones are all part of their own group,
and the soft zither samples are part of another group.

5. Click on an empty part of the Key Range area to deselect all the zones. On your CD-ROM, browse to NNXT > NNXT Samples > zither > zither chopsticks. Select all 15 samples in the Zither Chopsticks folder and click OK. Then select Group Selected Zones from the Edit menu or from the Context menu. Now you should have three groups: zither soft, zither loud, and zither chopsticks. This will come in handy for selecting the groups when you begin assigning velocity ranges and velocity crossfades.

6. If you played a key on your keyboard right now, you would hear a huge (loud) mess because, by default, all 45 samples are mapped to all the keys between C1 and C6 and would be triggered simultaneously. This is not what we want! From the Edit menu, click on Select All Zones, and then select Automap Zones from the Edit menu. Since root key information has been included in the sample files, you will see that all the samples are mapped quite nicely across the keyboard (see Figure 3.30).

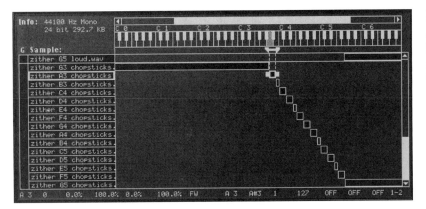

Figure 3.30

After applying Automap Zones, all the samples are mapped quite nicely across the keyboard.

7. Click on an empty part of the Key Range area to deselect all the zones. Click in the Group area to the left of the chopsticks zones to select the zither chopsticks group. If necessary, first drag the vertical scroll bar down so you can see this group.

8. Now that all the zones in the zither chopsticks group are selected, set the Lo Velocity knob to a value of 110. Now the zither chopsticks samples will not be triggered unless you hit the keys pretty hard.

9. To make this perform more like a real zither, some adjustments must be made in the Amp Envelope section. From the Edit menu, click on Select All Zones. Set the Amp Envelope so that Attack = off (0), Hold = off (0), Decay = 10.6 seconds, Sustain = 0, and Release = 10 seconds. Set the Spread amount to 54%. The Spread mode should be set to Key, which approximates the stereo image of an acoustic piano, with the low keys on the left and the high keys on the right of the stereo image. Since these samples are played rather high on the keyboard (G3-G5), and are therefore all on the right side of the stereo image, adjust the Pan knob to a value of −30%. This will put the zither in the middle of the stereo image, with the low strings toward the right and the high strings toward the left (see Figure 3.31).

Figure 3.31

The Amplifier Envelope section should look like this by the end of Step 9.

10. With all zones still selected, set the Level knob in the Velocity section to 33% (see Figure 3.32). Now when you play a little harder, things will get a little louder.

93

Figure 3.32

With all zones selected, set the Level knob in the Velocity section to 33% so that the volume will be affected by how hard you play.

11. Click on an empty part of the Key Range area to deselect all the zones. Click in the zither soft Group area to select all the zither soft zones. Set the Hi Velocity knob to 109. You will see the selected zones are now shaded with diagonal lines because the velocity range is no longer full. Set the Fade Out knob to 76 (see Figure 3.33). Now the zither soft zones will begin to fade out the harder you strike the keys (at velocities higher than 76).

Figure 3.33

Set the Fade Out knob to 76 so that the zither soft zones will begin to fade out the harder you strike the keys (at velocities higher than 76).

12. Click on an empty part of the Key Range area to deselect all the zones. Click in the zither loud Group area to select all the zither loud zones. Set the Lo Velocity knob to 76 and the Hi Velocity knob to 109. Then set the Fade In knob to a value of 105. Now velocities above 105 will trigger these zones at their full volume, and lower velocities will fade in as they approach 105. You have just created a velocity crossfade.

13. Let's set volume levels for the three groups. Click on an empty part of the Key Range area to deselect all the zones. The Amp level for the zither soft group can stay at the default setting of 0.0 dB. Select the zither loud group and set the Amp level to 3.9 dB. Then select the zither chopsticks group and set the Amp Level knob to 7 dB.

14. There is no crossfade between the zither loud group and the zither chopsticks group. At velocities of 110–127, the only group triggered will be the zither chopsticks group. I noticed that the bottom five zither chopsticks samples were jumping out a little more loudly than I'd like. Click on an empty part of the Key Range area to deselect all the zones. Select zither C5 chopsticks in the Sample area, and then turn the Amp Level knob down to about 4.2 dB. Then set zither D5 chopsticks Amp level to 6.4 dB, zither E5 chopsticks Amp level to 3.8 dB, and set zither F5 chopsticks and zither G5 chopsticks Amp level to about 4.2 dB. If you click in the Group area to select the entire group, you will see a little M for "multiple" next to the Amp Level knob to show that multiple values for this parameter exist within the current selections.

15. Two final easy steps: In the upper-left corner of the Remote Editor, turn the Key Polyphony up to 16. Then, on the Main Panel, turn on High Quality Interpolation.

I have saved this exercise in the NN-XT Patches folder with the name Velocity Zither. You should be able to play this patch pretty expressively. Since your loudest notes will trigger the bouncing chopsticks samples, it can sound like you are playing a high-pitched hammer dulcimer. An example of this is saved in the NN-XT In Action folder, also with the name Velocity Zither.

WHY DESELECT ALL ZONES BEFORE LOADING NEW SAMPLES?

In the preceding exercise, I instructed you to click on an empty part of the Key Range area to deselect all the zones before opening the Sample Browser to load a new group of samples. This was necessary because, otherwise, you would have been unable to load a new group of samples. There is a reason for this. Whenever one sample has Edit Focus, when you try to load a new sample, it will replace the sample in the zone with Edit Focus. This is by design. If you try to load a group of samples while a zone has Edit Focus, you will be unable to do so. The OK button in the Sample Browser will be grayed out because you cannot load a group of samples into a single zone. One sample per zone, maximum! Unless you are actually trying to replace a sample in a specific zone, it is good to get in the habit of deselecting all zones before loading new samples. It is easy to lose track of which zone has Edit Focus, and then wonder where the sample you just loaded ended up!

Group Parameters

The Group parameters affect entire groups rather than individual zones (see Figure 3.34). Even if you have only selected one zone, all the zones in the entire group to which the selected zone belongs will be affected when adjusting any of the Group parameters. You can set several groups to the same value by selecting at least one zone in each group you would like to adjust, and then change the setting of the desired Group parameter. The following Group parameters are available:

Figure 3.34

Changes to the Group parameters affect entire groups rather than individual zones.

- **Key Poly**—The Key Polyphony setting determines the number of keys that you can play at one time, with a maximum available setting of 99 and a minimum of 1, which would render the group monophonic. Although in other samplers and synths, polyphony often refers to the number of voices that can be played at one time, the NN-XT's Key Polyphony setting determines the number of keys that can be played simultaneously, regardless of how many voices each key triggers. Keep in mind that a key you have struck still continues playing even after you let go if you have a long Amp Envelope Release setting, and it continues to count against your Key Polyphony setting until the end of the Release portion of the Amp Envelope.

95

- **Legato/Retrig**—The Legato setting is designed to work with monophonic sounds. In Legato mode, if the Key Polyphony is set to 1 (monophonic), when you hold down a key and then press another key without releasing the previous, the pitch will change, but the envelopes will not retrigger, so you will not hear a new Attack when the second key is pressed. If the Key Polyphony is set to more than 1 voice, then Legato will only be applied when the number of keys specified by the Key Poly setting are "used up." For example, if you had a Key Polyphony setting of 3 and you held down a three-note chord, the next note you played would be Legato (no Attack). Also, this fourth Legato key in the example will cause one of the keys in the three-note chord to stop sounding because all the assigned keys were already used up.

- **Retrig**—This is the setting you will normally choose for playing polyphonic patches (patches with a Key Poly setting higher than 1). In Retrig mode, when you strike a key without releasing the previous key, the envelopes are retriggered the same way as when you release all the keys and then strike a new key. In monophonic mode (Key Poly setting of 1), Retrig has the following additional effect: If you press a key, hold it, press a new key, and then release it while still holding down the fist key, the first key will be retriggered. This can be used for "hammer-on" or pivot effects.

- **LFO 1 Rate**—This is used for controlling the rate of LFO 1 if LFO 1 is set for Group Rate mode. In that case, this knob will override the Rate parameter in the LFO 1 section. For more about this, please refer to the LFO 1 portion of the following "Synth Parameters" section of this chapter.

- **Portamento**—The Portamento setting determines the amount of time it takes to "glide" in pitch from one note to the next. The default setting of zero results in zero effect, and the farther you turn the knob to the right, the longer it takes to glide from one note to the next. Although it's a pretty straightforward feature, you can find more details regarding Portamento in Chapter 1, "The Subtractor." Note that in Legato mode, you will only hear the portamento effect when playing legato (tied) notes.

WHAT'S THAT LITTLE "M" NEXT TO MY KNOB?

The Group parameters, the Synth parameters, and the Multiple Adjustment Sample parameters can all be set differently for different zones or groups. When several zones or groups are selected in the Key Map display that contain different settings for a given parameter, that parameter will have a little letter M (for Multiple) displayed next to it to indicate that the currently shown value of the parameter only applies to some, but not all, of the currently selected zones or groups (see Figure 3.35). In the case of conflicting values, the value shown will be the value that applies to the zone with Edit Focus.

Figure 3.35

A little letter M (for Multiple) displayed next to a parameter indicates that the currently shown value of the parameter only applies to some, but not all, of the currently selected zones or groups.

Synth Parameters

The Synth parameters are used to shape the sound of your samples (see Figure 3.36). Changes to these parameters apply to all selected zones, regardless of Edit Focus. These parameters can be adjusted and applied individually to any or all of the zones in your patch simultaneously. This means that unlike the NN-19, in which only a single setting for the Synth parameters could be made, the NN-XT can have completely different Synth parameter settings for each zone. We will be working (more or less) counterclockwise through the NN-XT's Synth parameters.

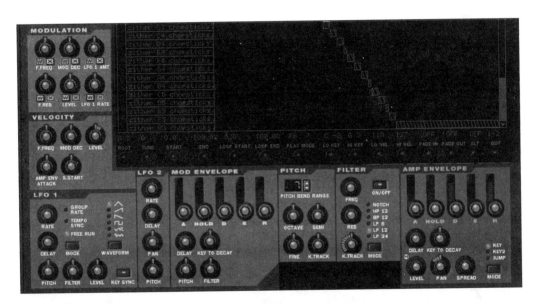

Figure 3.36

The Synth parameters are used to shape the sound of your samples.
Changes to these parameters apply to all selected zones, regardless of Edit Focus.

Amp Envelope Section

The Amp Envelope section of the NN-XT (see Figure 3.37) does the old ADSR Envelope (see Chapter 1) one better with the addition of the Hold parameter, which freezes the sound at its maximum amplitude for a little while before the Decay portion of the envelope begins. This feature is unique to the NN-XT. (It does not appear on any of the other Reason Instruments.)

Here is a rundown of the Amp Envelope:

- **Attack**—The amount of time it takes for the amplitude of a sound to climb from zero to its peak level.

- **Hold**—The amount of time the sound will remain at its peak amplitude before beginning the Decay portion of the envelope.

- **Decay**—The amount of time it takes for the amplitude of a sound to fall from its peak level to the level determined by the Sustain parameter, assuming you keep holding down the key(s).

- **Sustain**—At the end of a note's decay, the Sustain value determines the level at which the amplitude rests as long as the note is being held.

- **Release**—The amount of time it takes for the level of a sound to drop to zero from whatever level it was when you let go of a note.

Figure 3.37

The NN-XT's Amp Envelope section.

In addition to the actual AHDSR Envelope knobs, the following controls are included in the Amp Envelope:

- **Delay**—This control is used to create a delay between when a note is played and when the Amp Envelope actually takes effect.

- **Key to Decay**—This bipolar control is used to offset the Amp Decay setting, depending on where on the keyboard you play. Turning the knob to the right will cause the Decay value to be raised the higher up on the keyboard you play. Turning the knob to the left will cause the Decay value to be lowered the higher up on the keyboard you play. Setting the knob in the center position causes the parameter to have no effect.

- **Level**—This control sets the volume level for the selected zone.

- **Pan**—This control is used to adjust the stereo balance of the output pair to which the selected zone is routed.

- **Spread**—This controls how far left and right the notes will be spread out in the stereo image. (It controls the width of the stereo image.) The type of spread you wish to apply is determined by the Mode button.

- **Mode**—Determines the type of stereo spread you would like to apply.

The three Spread modes, which can be chosen with the Mode button are as follows:

■ **Key**—This is the most natural pan setting for piano samples. The pan position shifts gradually from left to right the higher up on the keyboard you play.

■ **Key 2**—This setting shifts the pan position from left to right in eight steps for each consecutively higher key you play, and then repeats the cycle.

■ **Jump**—This setting alternates the pan position from left to right for each note played, even if you are playing the same note over and over again.

Filter Section

The NN-XT has just one filter, which is nearly identical to the filters found on the Subtractor (see Figure 3.38). The NN-XT's Filter section has the following controls:

Figure 3.38

The Filter section of the NN-XT.

■ **Freq**—The Filter Frequency knob (also known as the *cutoff filter*) specifies where in the audio frequency spectrum the filter's effect will be focused. It determines the cutoff frequency. The cutoff frequency (in the case of a High Pass or Low Pass filter) is simply the frequency at which the filter begins to take effect. So in a High Pass Filter, for example, the cutoff frequency will be the frequency at which the filter begins cutting off (or filtering out) low frequencies, while allowing high frequencies to pass through. In the case of a Notch or Band Pass filter, the value of the Filter Frequency knob sets the frequency at which the filter has the greatest effect, even though the filter will still be affecting a range of frequencies immediately above *and* below the cutoff frequency.

■ **Res**—In the case of High Pass and Low Pass filters, the Resonance knob is used to emphasize the frequencies around the cutoff frequency specified by the Filter Frequency knob. This is achieved (internally) by feeding back the output signal of the Filter into the Filter input. The Resonance knob then controls the amount of feedback. In the case of the Band Pass and Notch filters, the Resonance knob determines the bandwidth. High Resonance settings will result in a narrower bandwidth (fewer frequencies above and below the cutoff frequency are affected), and low Resonance settings will result in a wider bandwidth (more frequencies above and below the cutoff frequency are affected).

- ■ **K.Track**—The Filter Keyboard Tracking knob determines to what extent (if any) the filter frequency is affected by which notes are played on your MIDI keyboard. When the Filter Keyboard Tracking knob is turned up, playing higher notes will result in higher Filter Frequency settings, while playing lower notes will result in lower Filter Frequency settings. This is not a bipolar control, although there is a visible notch at the center position. This is to draw attention to the fact that the Filter Keyboard Tracking control is designed so that setting the knob to the center position results in the filter frequency being adjusted in such a way that the harmonic content of the sound remains consistent across the keyboard.

- ■ **Filter On/Off**—This button is used to activate or deactivate the Filter section.

- ■ **Mode**—The Filter Mode button selects from among six filters (see Figure 3.39).

Figure 3.39

The NN-XT has six Filter modes to choose from.

- • **Notch**—The Notch filter rejects mid-frequencies (determined by the Freq knob) and allows frequencies above and below that "notch" to pass through. The specific frequency at which the Notch filter's effect is concentrated is determined by the Filter Frequency knob, and the size (or *bandwidth*) of the notch is determined by the value of the Resonance knob.

- • **HP 12**—The 12-Decibel High Pass filter allows high frequencies to pass through but attenuates (by 12 decibels per octave) frequencies below the frequency determined by the Filter Frequency (or cutoff filter) knob.

- • **BP 12**—The Band Pass filter is the opposite of the Notch filter. While the Notch filter selects a band (or group of frequencies) to filter out while allowing all other frequencies to pass through, the Band Pass filter selects a band (or group of frequencies) to pass through, while filtering out (attenuating by 12 decibels per octave) frequencies above and below that band. As with the Notch filter, the specific frequency at which the Band Pass filter's effect is concentrated is determined by the value of the Filter Frequency knob, while the size of the frequency band (or *bandwidth*) is determined by the value of the Resonance knob.

- • **LP 6**—The 6-Decibel Low Pass filter allows low frequencies to pass through but filters high frequencies with an extra-soft roll-off curve of 6 decibels per octave. Note that this filter has no Resonance, so the Res knob will have no effect. The NN-XT is the only Reason device to feature a 6-dB Low Pass Filter.

- **LP 12**—The 12-Decibel Low Pass Filter allows low frequencies to pass through but filters high frequencies with a roll-off curve of 12 decibels per octave.

- **LP 24**—The 24-Decibel Low Pass Filter allows low frequencies to pass through but filters high frequencies with a more extreme roll-off curve of 24 decibels per octave.

Pitch Control Section

The Pitch Control Section of the NN-XT has a familiar feature set with added bonus functionality in the Keyboard Tracking department, which is unique to the NN-XT (see Figure 3.40). The Pitch Control section has the following controls:

- **Pitch Bend Range**—Controls the range of the Pitch Bend wheel for the currently selected zones. It has a maximum range of + or − 24 semitones (two octaves).

- **Octave**—Changes the pitch of the currently selected zones in octave increments. It can raise or lower the pitch by up to five octaves.

- **Semi**—Raises the pitch of the currently selected zones by up to 12 semitones (one octave) in semitone increments.

- **Fine**—Changes the pitch of the currently selected zones in one-cent increments. This parameter is bipolar and allows you to raise or lower the pitch by up to 50 cents.

- **K.Track**—The Pitch Keyboard Tracking control determines how much each key you play affects the pitch at which a zone plays back.

Figure 3.40

The Pitch Control section of the NN-XT.

Pitch Keyboard Tracking: A Closer Look

Unlike the NN-19 in which Pitch Keyboard Tracking is simply on or off, the NN-XT allows you to choose all points in between and beyond. When this control is all the way to the left, which key you play has no effect on the pitch at which the currently selected zones play back. As you turn the knob to the right, which key you play will gradually begin to have an effect, until you reach the default center (or "normal") position, where each key will shift the pitch one semitone up or down (just like playing a real piano in that regard). Settings to the right of center will cause pitch intervals between keys of greater than one semitone, with a maximum value of 1200 cents per key.

That's a one-octave change from one key to the next! The flexibility of this control on the NN-XT can produce some very interesting effects. This is explored in the following exercise.

1. Start with an empty rack and create an instance of the NN-XT.

2. Click on the NN-XT's Browse Patch button and load the Velocity Zither patch from the NN-XT Patches folder on your CD-ROM.

3. In the Pitch section, set the Octave knob to –2, set the Semi knob to 4, and set the Keyboard Tracking knob to 166 cent/key (see Figure 3.41). If you have trouble getting this exact value, try holding down the Shift key when you drag the knob. You also might try setting the Mouse Knob Range to Very Precise on the General page of the Reason Preferences.

Figure 3.41

Set the Octave knob to –2, set the Semi knob to 4, and set the Keyboard Tracking knob to 166 cent/key.

I have saved the above exercise as Detuned Zither in the NN-XT Patches folder on your CD-ROM. I have included a twisted example of how you might use this sort of sound if you are some kind of weirdo. The example song file is also called Detuned Zither and is saved in the NN-XT In Action folder on your CD-ROM.

Modulation Envelope Section

The Modulation Envelope, like the Amp Envelope, includes a Hold stage in the envelope, thus making it an AHDSR Envelope (see Figure 3.42). The Modulation Envelope can be routed to control the pitch of the selected zones, as well as the filter frequency. Its controls are as follows:

■ **Attack**—The amount of time it takes for the Modulation Amount to climb from zero to its peak level.

■ **Hold**—The amount of time the Modulation Amount will remain at its peak level before beginning the decay portion of the envelope.

■ **Decay**—The amount of time it takes for the Modulation Amount to fall from its peak level to the level determined by the Sustain parameter, assuming you keep holding down the key(s).

■ **Sustain**—At the end of the Modulation Envelope's decay, the Sustain value determines the level at which the Modulation Amount rests as long as a note is being held.

- **Release**—The amount of time it takes for the Modulation Amount to drop to zero from whatever level it was when you let go of a note.

- **Delay**—This control is used to create a delay between when a note is played and when the Modulation Envelope actually takes effect.

- **Key to Decay**—This bipolar control is used to offset the Modulation Decay setting, depending on where on the keyboard you play. Turning the knob to the right will cause the Decay value to be raised the higher up on the keyboard you play. Turning the knob to the left will cause the Decay value to be lowered the higher up on the keyboard you play. Setting the knob in the center position will have no effect.

- **Pitch**—This bipolar control determines how the Modulation Envelope will affect the pitch of the selected zones. The farther to the right the knob is turned, the more the pitch will be raised in response to the Modulation Envelope. The farther to the left the knob is turned, the more the pitch will be lowered in response to the Modulation Envelope. Like all bipolar controls, the center position means that the parameter will have no effect.

- **Filter**—This bipolar control determines how the Modulation Envelope will affect the filter frequency of the selected zones. The farther to the right the knob is turned, the more the filter frequency will be raised in response to the Modulation Envelope. The farther to the left the knob is turned, the more the filter frequency will be lowered in response to the Modulation Envelope. If you noticed that there is no dedicated Filter Envelope on the NN-XT, you should now be relieved to discover that the Modulation Envelope can be used as a perfectly good Filter Envelope!

Figure 3.42
The Modulation Envelope section.

The Modulation Envelope provides a great opportunity to get a solid feel for the AHDSR Envelope concept (and also to reinforce your understanding of the slightly simpler ADSR Envelope). So far in the course of this book, you have primarily used envelopes to control amplitude (volume) and filter frequency. In the following exercise, you will use the Modulation Envelope in the NN-XT to control pitch.

1. Start with an empty rack and create an instance of the NN-XT.

2. Click on the NN-XT's Browse Patch button and load Reason Factory Sound Bank > NN-XT Sampler Patches > Organ > Vox FluteMellow. I have chosen this because it is a simple sound with infinite sustain. Please play a few notes to become familiar with this sound.

3. Click the triangular button to the lower left of the Pitch Bend wheel to open the Remote Editor.

4. From the Edit menu, click Select All Zones. Now any changes you make to the Synth parameters will affect all the samples across the entire keyboard.

5. Turn the Amp Envelope Release knob up to about 12 seconds. To see this value, you must have Show Parameter Value Tool Tip checked on the General page of the Reason Preferences. Now play a few notes to hear the effect of the new Amp Envelope Release setting.

6. Turn all five Modulation Envelope knobs all the way down. Then turn up the Modulation Envelope to Pitch knob (simply labeled Pitch) to about 3 o'clock.

7. Slowly turn up the Modulation Envelope Attack knob, playing a key over and over as you go to hear the effect of the increasing Attack values. Set the Attack value to about 2.5 seconds. You will hear the somewhat slow attack, followed by instant decay. Remember the decay is also a measure of time, and the Decay is set to zero, so it takes no time at all for the pitch to fall back down to normal after the end of the Attack portion of the envelope.

8. Move the Modulation Envelope Hold knob up to a value of about two seconds. Now when you play and hold a note, you should hear the pitch rise to the top of the Attack cycle, and then hold for two seconds at its peak level (determined by the Modulation Envelope to Pitch knob) before its instant decay.

9. Set the Mod Envelope Decay knob to about 3 seconds (I set mine for 3.25 seconds). Now when you play and hold a note, you will hear the gradual attack, followed by a couple of seconds of hold, and then a gradual decay down to the original pitch.

10. Set the Mod Envelope Sustain knob to 50%. Remember that Sustain is the only parameter of the AHDSR Envelope that is not a function of time. Instead, it sets a level: in this case, the level at which the pitch value will rest at the end of the Decay portion of the envelope (as long as you continue to hold down a note). Since Release is set for zero, you will notice that when you let go of a note, the pitch immediately drops down to the original, unmodulated note. You can hear this because the Amp Envelope Release is turned up.

11. Finally, set the Mod Envelope Release knob to about 2.5 seconds. Now when you let go of a note, instead of an instant Mod Envelope Release (zero seconds), you will hear a gradual drop back down to the original pitch (see Figure 3.43).

Figure 3.43

The Modulation Envelope section should look like this when you are done with the exercise.

Even though this is a pretty simple (and not terribly beautiful) exercise, I have saved it as a Reason song file named ModEnvPitch in the NN-XT In Action folder on your CD-ROM, in case you want to check your work. I did not play anything into the Reason Sequencer in the example song, so you will have to play your own keyboard to hear the envelope.

LFO 1

The first of the NN-XT's two low-frequency oscillators has got the goods (see Figure 3.44). It also has a few surprises in among the usual LFO goodies. LFO 1 has the following controls:

Figure 3.44

LFO 1 has got the goods, including plenty of destinations and of waveforms.

- ■ **Rate**—The LFO 1 Rate knob controls the speed at which LFO 1 oscillates. The behavior of this knob is determined by the Mode (LFO 1 Sync Mode) setting.

- ■ **Mode**—The LFO 1 Sync mode has three possible settings. In Group Rate mode, the LFO 1 Rate knob is overridden by the LFO 1 Rate knob in the Group parameters section in the upper-left corner of the Remote Editor. In Tempo Sync mode, LFO 1 is synced to the track, playing at a speed set in relation to the tempo as set in the Reason Transport Panel. When Tempo Sync mode is activated, the Rate knob value is measured in musical note values, ranging from 1/64 to 1/32. In Free Run mode, the Rate knob value is measured in Hertz (cycles per second) and is not tied to the track tempo.

- **Delay**—The Delay control determines how much time will pass after striking a note before LFO 1 kicks in. At the default setting (all the way to the left), there is no delay and LFO 1 is engaged immediately.

- **Pitch**—The LFO 1 to Pitch knob determines to what extent LFO 1 will modulate the pitch for the currently selected zones. The control is bipolar, allowing LFO 1 to positively or negatively affect the Pitch parameter. Turning the knob to the right causes LFO 1 to positively affect pitch, and turning it left of center causes LFO 1 to negatively affect pitch. In the default center position, LFO 1 does not affect the filter frequency.

- **Filter**—The LFO 1 to Filter Frequency knob determines to what extent LFO 1 will modulate the filter frequency for the currently selected zones. The control is bipolar, allowing LFO 1 to positively or negatively affect the Filter Frequency parameter. In the default center position, LFO 1 does not affect the filter frequency.

- **Level**—The LFO 1 to Level knob determines to what extent LFO 1 will modulate the volume level of the Amp Envelope section for the currently selected zones. The control is bipolar, allowing LFO 1 to positively or negatively affect the Amp Level parameter. In the default center position, LFO 1 does not affect the amp level.

- **Key Sync**—When Key Sync is activated, LFO 1 is forced to restart its modulation cycle each time you strike a key. Note that Key Sync is "hardwired" into LFO 2, and there is no button with which to turn it off!

- **Waveform**—The LFO 1 Waveform selector allows you to choose from among the following five waveforms: Triangle, Inverse Sawtooth, Sawtooth, Square, Random, and Soft Random. For more information on the characteristics of these waveforms, please refer to Chapter 1.

LFO 2

LFO 2 is a fairly simple low-frequency oscillator (see Figure 3.45). It has only one waveform (Triangle), which makes it suitable for adding vibrato or tremolo effects.

Figure 3.45

LFO 2 is a fairly simple low-frequency oscillator, well-suited for vibrato and tremolo effects.

- **Rate**—The LFO 2 Rate knob controls the speed at which LFO 2 oscillates.

- **Delay**—The Delay control determines how much time will pass after striking a note before LFO 2 kicks in. At the default setting (all the way to the left), there is no delay, and LFO 2 is engaged immediately. This can be a nice effect if you want a moment of steady note before you apply vibrato.

- **Pan**—This is a destination control that routes LFO 2 to the Stereo Pan control in the Amp Envelope section. You can use this to create some great stereo tremolo effects, which can sound especially cool on Rhodes piano, a la Pink Floyd. The control is bipolar, and the Triangle wave that LFO 2 uses appears to be bipolar as well. If you have the Amp section Pan knob dead center, setting the LFO 2 to Pan knob hard left or right will cause the sound to sweep all the way to the left and all the way to the right in the stereo image either way. However, with the LFO 2 to Pan knob set to the right, the sound will start on the right before sweeping left, while setting the knob to the left will cause the sound to start on the left before sweeping right. Since LFO 2 automatically uses Key Sync, this process retriggers every time you hit a key, instead of continuing uninterrupted as a classic tremolo or vibrato effect would. This is most noticeable when doing stereo pans, which are slow enough that you can easily notice which side they start on.

- **Pitch**—This is a destination control that routes LFO 2 to modulate pitch.

Velocity Section

The Velocity section (see Figure 3.46) allows you to determine how velocity (how hard you play a note) will affect any or all of the following five parameters:

- **Filter Frequency**—This bipolar control adjusts the manner in which how hard you strike a key affects the Filter Frequency parameter. Positive values will result in higher velocities causing higher filter frequency values. This can be used to add realism, since many instruments sound brighter when played harder.

- **Modulation Decay**—This bipolar control adjusts the manner in which how hard you strike a key affects the Decay portion of the Modulation Envelope. Positive values mean that playing harder will result in longer Modulation Envelope Decay times, while negative settings will result in higher velocities, causing shorter Modulation Envelope Decay times.

- **Amp Level**—This bipolar control adjusts the extent to which how hard you strike a key affects how loud or soft the selected zones will play back. If this feature is used, it is normally assigned a positive value, since a negative value would mean that the harder you play, the quieter you sound, which would be weird, right?

- **Amp Envelope Attack**—A positive value for this bipolar parameter means that the harder you play, the slower the Amp Envelope Attack will be (the more time it will take for a note to fade in). A negative value will result in higher velocities, causing a faster Amp Envelope Attack.

■ **Sample Start**—A positive value for this bipolar parameter means that the harder you play, the farther along in the sample playback will begin. In other words, the harder you play, the less of the attack you will hear. Negative values mean that the harder you play, the more of the attack you will hear; but in order to use negative values, you have to first increase the value of the Sample Start knob in the Sample parameters section.

Figure 3.46
The Velocity section allows you to determine how any of several parameters will be affected by how hard you strike a note.

Modulation Control Section

The Modulation Control section is used to route and control how the signal from both the Modulation wheel and from External Control (breathe, expression pedal, or aftertouch) will affect various NN-XT parameters (see Figure 3.47). Each of the knobs in the Modulation Control section can be used to control Mod wheel, External Control, or both, by clicking the little W and X buttons below the knobs. When the W is selected (lit up green), the knob will be used to route the signal from the Mod wheel. When the X button is engaged, the knob will affect the extent to which External Control will modulate the given parameter. It is possible to select both the W and X buttons for a given parameter so that both the Mod wheel and External Control routing are adjusted simultaneously by the same knob. These knobs adjust whether the Mod wheel or External Control will have a positive or negative effect on the given parameter, and they adjust the amount of modulation the Mod wheel or External Control can apply to the following six parameters.

Figure 3.47
The Modulation Control section is used to route and control how the signal from the Modulation wheel and from the External Control (breathe, expression pedal, or aftertouch) will affect various NN-XT parameters.

■ **Filter Frequency**—This bipolar control routes virtual control voltage from the Mod wheel, External Control, or both to modulate the NN-XT's Filter Frequency parameter.

■ **Filter Resonance**—This bipolar control routes virtual control voltage from the Mod wheel, External Control, or both to modulate the NN-XT's Filter Resonance parameter.

- **Modulation Decay**—This bipolar control routes virtual control voltage from the Mod wheel, External Control, or both to modulate the Decay parameter of the Modulation Envelope.

- **Amp Level**—This bipolar control routes virtual control voltage from the Mod wheel, External Control, or both to modulate the Amp Level parameter of the Amp Envelope section.

- **LFO 1 Amount**—This bipolar control routes virtual control voltage from the Mod wheel, External Control, or both to modulate the LFO 1 Amount parameter.

- **LFO 1 Rate**—This bipolar control routes virtual control voltage from the Mod wheel, External Control, or both to modulate the LFO 1 Rate parameter.

Sick Fun with Samples

The following patch is pretty crazy and shows you what a long, strange trip you can take from Point A (the original sample) to Point B (what it sounds like after applying some Synth parameters). Warning: This patch has the potential to get super loud. It has a slow feedback element that can melt your brain. Therefore, I am not kidding when I suggest that you put it through a compressor!

1. Start with an empty rack and create an instance of the MClass Compressor, followed by the NN-XT. The default setting on the MClass Compressor should afford barely sufficient ear protection. Turn on High Quality Interpolation on the NN-XT as a matter of course.

2. Open the Remote Editor, click the Load Sample button, and load zither A3 chopsticks.wav from the NN-XT Samples > zither > zither chopsticks folder on your CD-ROM.

3. From the Edit menu, select Duplicate Zones. Do this three times so that you have four identical zones (see Figure 3.48).

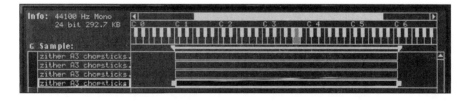

Figure 3.48

Select Duplicate Zones from the Edit menu three times so that you have four identical zones.

4. Click in the Group area (to the left of the Sample area) to select the whole group (all four zones) and drag the left boundary handle all the way to the left (see Figure 3.49).

5. With all the zones still selected, set the Amp Envelope so that Attack = 0.52 seconds, Hold = off (0), Decay = 60 milliseconds, Sustain = 0 dB, and Release = 0.75 seconds.

6. With all the zones still selected, set the Filter mode to LP 24 (24-dB Low Pass). The Freq knob should be all the way up. Set the Filter Resonance knob to 58%, and set the Filter Keyboard Tracking knob to its center position.

109

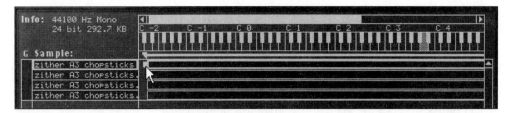

Figure 3.49

Select the whole group (all four zones) and drag the left boundary handle all the way to the left. In the screenshot, I am dragging the left boundary handle in the Key Range area, but you could also click and drag the left boundary handle in the Tab Bar area above.

7. With all the zones still selected, set the Mod Envelope so that Attack = 1.64 seconds, Hold = off (0), Decay = maximum, Sustain = 0, and Release = maximum. Set the Filter (Mod Env to Filter Freq) knob to about −83%.

8. Click on an empty part of the Key Range area to deselect all zones. Then click on the first (topmost) zone to select it. In the Pitch section, set the Fine control to −5 cents. Then in the Amp Envelope section, turn the Pan knob all the way to the left.

9. Click on the second zone to select it. In the Pitch section, set the Fine control to 5 cents. Then in the Amp Envelope section, turn the Pan knob all the way to the right. You should now have a noticeably wider stereo image.

10. Click on the third zone to select it. Set the Play Mode knob to FW-Loop. Then turn the Loop End knob to the left until you have set a value of 0.8% (see Figure 3.50). In the Pitch section, set the Fine control to −5 cents. Then in the Amp Envelope section, set the Pan knob to a value of −60%.

11. Click on the fourth zone to select it. Set the Play Mode knob to FW-Loop. Then turn the Loop End knob to the left until you have set a value of 1.0%. In the Pitch section, set the Fine control to 5 cents. Then in the Amp Envelope section, set the Pan knob to a value of 60%.

Figure 3.50

Turn the Loop End knob to the left until you have set a value of 0.8%.

I have saved this patch in the NN-XT Patches folder with the name SciFi Zither. When you play this patch, you will hear an initial sound (with a filter sweep), and then if you continue to hold down the keys, you will hear another tone fade in. If you keep holding down the keys, you will hear the eventually excruciating (but kind of cool) feedback sound I mentioned. It is especially brutal on the higher keys and may require turning down the Master Volume on the NN-XT if you plan to play the really high keys. I really like the way it fades in on the lower keys. If you want to lose the first sound and use only the slow-onset second sound, you can easily achieve this by selecting all zones and then simply turning the Mod Envelope Attack all the way down. I have saved it that way as well with the name EndOfTheWorld Zither. These sounds are a bit weird, but I hope they give you a taste of the nearly limitless power the NN-XT has to offer when it comes to shaping your samples.

So what about that crazy feedback anyway? What did we do? Why does the SciFi Zither sound that way? The initial filter sweep is due to the Mod Envelope modulating the Filter Frequency parameter. The relationship is interesting because it is an inverse relationship. Remember the Filter Envelope Invert buttons on the Subtractor and the Malström? We did basically the same thing here. The Modulation Envelope is in every way our Filter Envelope in this patch, and in turning the bipolar Mod Envelope to Filter Frequency knob down to −83%, we have inverted the envelope! The Mod Envelope Attack is set at about 1.6 seconds, long enough to go "eeeeeoooowww." If the envelope were not inverted (and the filter frequency were set much lower), it would go "uuoooaaaeeeee." It helps if you actually make those noises out loud, especially if you are in a library. As the envelope reaches its maximum amplitude at the end of the attack, this turns the filter frequency down so low you really can't hear it anymore until that *other* sound starts fading in.

So what about that other sound? The inverted Decay portion of the Mod Envelope is set at maximum, which is about 200 seconds. As the Decay portion of the Mod Envelope slowly progresses, the filter frequency is very slowly increased. (It increases instead of decreasing because the envelope is inverted.) That's why the sound fades back in. The Sustain setting on the Amp Envelope is at maximum, so as long as you keep holding down the keys, you will still be able to hear any audible signal that has made it as far as the Amp Envelope. But what about that feedback? That is related to the Filter Resonance setting. Remember that in a Low Pass filter (such as we are using) or in a High Pass filter, the Resonance parameter actually controls the amount of the filter's output signal that will be fed back to its input. So this patch actually has a pretty crazy resonant feedback loop built in.

NN-XT Rear Panel Connections

Please flip your Reason rack around by pressing the Tab key on your computer keyboard. As you can see, the NN-XT has an extensive Audio Output section in addition to an ample complement of control voltage inputs (see Figure 3.51).

Figure 3.51

The rear panel of the NN-XT.

Audio Outputs

The NN-XT has eight stereo output pairs (see Figure 3.51). The default left and right outputs are labeled Output 1/L, 2/R. Any zone (which in turn means any sample) loaded into the NN-XT can be assigned individually to any of these output pairs. I say "pairs," assuming you are using stereo samples. Obviously, this is not always the case! If you are using mono samples, you actually have up to 16 separate outputs to choose from. All you have to do is set the Amp Envelope Pan so that the eight zones assigned to the odd-numbered output channels are panned all the way left, and the other eight zones assigned to the even-numbered output channels are panned all the way right. That sounds like a good idea. Let's try that!

1. Start with an empty rack and create an instance of reMix, followed by the NN-XT.

2. Press the Tab key on your computer keyboard to flip the Reason rack around. You will see that by default, NN-XT Output 1/L, 2/R are connected to Channel 1 of reMix. Since you will be using mono samples and assigning them to individual outputs, click (and hold) on the cable where it connects to reMix Channel 1 Right Audio Input (the bottom cable) and drag to connect it to the Channel 2 Left (Mono) Input (see Figure 3.52).

Figure 3.52

Click (and hold) on the cable where it connects to reMix Channel 1 Right Audio Input, then drag to connect it to the Channel 2 Left (Mono) Input.

3. Now connect NN-XT Outputs 3 through 14 to reMix Left (mono) Audio Inputs 3 through 14 (see Figure 3.53).

4. Flip the rack back around facing front. Open the NN-XT Remote Editor, and click the Load Sample button to open the Sample Browser.

Figure 3.53

Connect NN-XT Outputs 3 through 14 to reMix Left (mono) Audio Inputs 3 through 14.

5. On your CD-ROM, browse to NN-XT > NN-XT Samples > Zither > Zither Soft. Then Shift-select all but the bottom (G5) sample and click OK.

6. Right-click (Ctrl-click, Mac) on the NN-XT and select Automap Zones. Now you should have 14 samples mapped individually to keys G3 through F5.

7. Click in a blank area of the Key Map display to deselect all the zones. Then click on the top sample (zither G3 soft.wav) and set its low key to G3. You can either do this by turning the Lo Key knob or by dragging the left boundary handle to the G3 key on the virtual keyboard (see Figure 3.54). Now the sample will not play below its root key of G3.

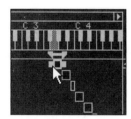

Figure 3.54

Click and drag the left boundary handle to the G3 key on the virtual keyboard so that the sample will not play below its root key of G3. You may have to use the horizontal scroll bar to find the left boundary handle. Or you could simply use the Lo Key knob.

8. As you can see by looking above the Out knob at the lower right of the Key Map display, this sample's Out is already assigned to 1–2. Now in the Amp Envelope section, set the Pan knob all the way to the left so that this zone will only be routed through Output 1 of the NN-XT.

9. Now select the second sample (zither A3 soft.wav) and set the Pan all the way to the right so that this zone will only be routed through Output 2 of the NN-XT.

10. Select the third sample (zither B3 soft.wav) and use the Out knob at the lower right of the Key Map display to set the Output for 3–4. Then set the Pan all the way to the left so that this zone will only be routed through Output 3 of the NN-XT.

11. Continue this until you have routed all 14 samples to all 14 outputs of the NN-XT, with the odd-numbered samples panned all the way left, and the even-numbered samples panned all the way right. Now when you play the white keys G3 through F5, each key will light up a different channel on reMix. By the way, to avoid any confusion, please set the F5 sample (which is the last sample and should be panned hard right and assigned to NN-XT Out 14) so that its high key is F5.

I have saved this exercise as Output Routing in the NN-XT In Action folder on your CD-ROM. If you are listening though headphones, you might hear some little birdies on a few of these zither soft samples. No extra charge. I usually fumigate for birds before recording soft instrument samples in my home studio, but it was such a pretty spring day, and the birds seemed so happy....

CV Inputs

The NN-XT does not have any control voltage outputs. However, it does have the following array of inputs for receiving control voltage signals from other Reason devices (see Figure 3.55).

Figure 3.55

The control voltage inputs on the rear panel of the NN-XT.

- **Sequencer Control**—These inputs allow you to control the NN-XT with an external mono-phonic device such as the Matrix. The Gate input receives Note On/Off values, as well as a Level value, which is similar to a Velocity value. The CV input receives note pitch informa-tion. These inputs are mono, which means they control only a single voice in the NN-XT.

- **Modulation Inputs**—These CV inputs allow you to control the following five NN-XT parameters with control voltage signals from other Reason devices: Osc (sample) Pitch, Filter Cutoff, Filter Resonance, LFO 1 Rate, Master Volume level (Main Panel), Stereo Pan, and Mod wheel. Each of these five control voltage inputs has a voltage Trim knob to boost or attenuate the incoming CV signal.

- **Gate Inputs**—These inputs allow you to trigger the Amp Envelope and Filter Envelope with CV signals. Connecting these inputs will override the normal triggering of the envelopes (from playing your keyboard or MIDI sequence).

4 Redrum

Redrum has a familiar look reminiscent of classic drum machines such as the Roland TR808 or 909. Like these classic drum machines, Redrum offers step programming with a row of 16 Step buttons. Unlike those old drum machines, Redrum is infinitely flexible, allowing you to load as many different sounds as there are Wave and AIFF files in the world (well, not all at the same time). You can mix and match samples to create your own drum kits, which you can then save as Redrum patches. You can instantly create fully random drum patterns, which can serve as starting points for your creative process. Once you get into Redrum, you will find it is easy to use and an essential tool for producing electronic music with Reason (see Figure 4.1).

Figure 4.1
Redrum carries on the spirit of the classic drum machines, but with its own style
and the nearly infinite sound and editing options of a virtual instrument.

Loading Kits and Individual Samples

Redrum patches load like any patch in any Reason device (see Figure 4.2). Redrum patches are complete drum kits (or sound kits, if you have created some sound effects kits). Not only do Redrum patches load samples into each of Redrum's 10 drum channels, but they also load channel strip settings. This is important to keep in mind. If you are working with one kit, and you have all your pan, pitch, and tone settings the way you want them, you'd better save that as a new patch, or else when you load another kit, those settings will be lost. If you do accidentally load another patch before saving the current settings, simply remain calm and select Undo Load Patch from the Edit menu. Then you will have a chance to save those settings. Patches (drum kits) are saved (as usual) by clicking the diskette icon to the far right of the Patch Browser window.

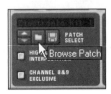

Figure 4.2

Click the Browse Patch button to load a new kit into Redrum.

Samples can be loaded on individual Redrum channels by clicking the Browse Sample button with the folder icon on it (see Figure 4.3). Any AIFF, Wave, SoundFont, or Rex file slice at any bit depth or sample rate, stereo or mono, may be used. You can scroll up and down through samples in the current folder with the up/down arrows to the left of the Browse Sample button. To hear the currently loaded sample, click the Trigger Drum button located to the right of the Mute and Solo buttons (see Figure 4.4). You can see and choose from all the samples in the current folder by clicking in the Sample Display window (see Figure 4.5), and you can also select Open Browser from that pop-up menu if you wish to open the Sample Browser.

Figure 4.3

Click the Browse Sample button to load a new sample into a Redrum channel.

Figure 4.4

To hear the currently loaded sample, click the Trigger Drum button.

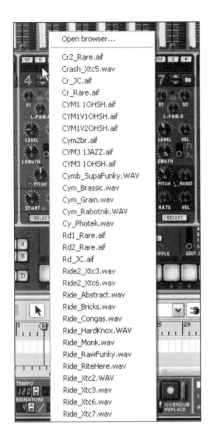

Figure 4.5

You can choose from among all the samples in the current folder by clicking in the Sample Display window.

Working with Patterns

Redrum can be played with a MIDI controller or the Reason Sequencer, just like any of the other Reason instruments. But part of the real fun of Redrum is using it like a drum machine, and that means creating using Redrum's built-in pattern-based programmer (see Figure 4.6). When creating patterns this way, each step in the pattern is represented by one of Redrum's 16 Step buttons. When Redrum is running (playing), little red LEDs will light up from left to right as each step is played. To place a drum hit on one of the steps, click on the corresponding Step button (see Figure 4.7). To choose which drum you are editing (which drum will sound when a Step button is activated), click the Select button for the channel the desired drum is on (see Figure 4.8).

Figure 4.6

Redrum's built-in pattern-based programmer emulates the look and feel of a classic drum machine.

Figure 4.7

To place a drum hit on one of the steps in your
drum pattern, click on the corresponding Step button.

Figure 4.8

To choose which drum you are editing in the pattern-based programmer,
click the Select button for the channel the desired drum is on.

Run/Enable Pattern Section/Pattern Enable

The Run button is used to start and stop playback of Redrum's Pattern section. When the Enable
Pattern Section button is engaged, the Run button will automatically engage whenever you press
Play on the Reason Transport Panel (see Figure 4.9). You can also click the Run button at any
time, whether your Reason song is playing or not. In either case, when Run is engaged, you will
see the Step lights move from left to right. If the sounds in Redrum are going to be triggered by
the Reason Sequencer, a MIDI controller, or a CV device (instead of using the Pattern section),
then you will want to turn off the Enable Pattern Section option. If Enable Pattern Section is
turned off, clicking the Run button will have no effect.

Figure 4.9

The Run button is used to start and stop playback of Redrum's Pattern section.
When the Enable Pattern Section button is engaged, the Run button will automatically engage
whenever you press Play on the Reason Transport Panel. If Enable Pattern Section is turned off,
clicking the Run button will have no effect.

In order to actually hear any patterns you have created, you must also engage the Pattern Enable
button (see Figure 4.10). This button (merely labeled Pattern) mutes and unmutes pattern playback
starting on the next downbeat, according to the time signature selected in the Reason Transport
Panel. This is a useful feature when you have more than one Redrum in your rack and want to
bring them in and out of the mix alternately.

Figure 4.10

The Pattern Enable button mutes and unmutes pattern playback starting on the next
downbeat, according to the time signature selected in the Reason Transport Panel.

Selecting Patterns

If the Enable Pattern Section button, the Pattern Enable button, and the Run button are all engaged, and you have loaded a drum kit into Redrum, you still will not hear anything unless you have already created a pattern and that pattern is currently selected. This is because all the patterns and pattern banks are empty by default. There are four pattern banks (A, B, C, and D), and each bank contains eight patterns, selectable by clicking your mouse on the numeric keypad (see Figure 4.11). When a new pattern is selected, the pattern change will take effect on the next downbeat. Pattern changes can be automated by recording them in the Reason Sequencer (just like any other automation, such as turning a knob or moving the Mod wheel one of the Reason synths). No pattern data is saved with the Redrum patch. Pattern data is saved with the Reason song file. It can also be saved within a Combinator patch.

Figure 4.11

Redrum has four pattern banks (A, B, C, and D), and each bank contains eight patterns, selectable by clicking your mouse on the numeric keypad.

Selecting Patterns with Your Computer Keyboard

In addition to using your mouse, you can also select patterns and pattern banks (and the Pattern Mute switch) with your computer keyboard. This is some advanced functionality, so if you just want to get on with learning how to make some beats, you can skip ahead to the "Pattern Length/Edit Steps" section and come back to this later. It's super easy, though!

Since the patterns are numbered 1 through 8, it makes sense to me to use the numbers 1 through 8 on your computer keyboard (the ones directly above QWERTY, *not* the Numeric keypad, which is reserved for the Transport controls). If you wanted to, you could instead use any other keys except for the spacebar, Tab, Enter, or the Numeric keypad. Numbers 1 through 8 will be used in this exercise.

1. With Redrum selected in your Reason device rack, select Keyboard Control Edit mode from the Options menu. This will reveal all parameters that can be controlled with the computer keyboard by placing yellow arrows over them (see Figure 4.12).

2. Double-click on the arrow over the Pattern 1 button. The arrow will turn into a twirling square.

3. Press the number 1 on your computer keyboard, and you will see that it has been assigned to the Pattern 1 button (see Figure 4.13).

4. Repeat this process for the remaining seven Pattern buttons (using the number 2 key for Pattern 2, the number 3 key for Pattern 3, and so on). When you are done, all eight Pattern buttons should be assigned to number 1 through 8 on your computer keyboard.

Figure 4.12

Selecting Keyboard Control Edit mode from the Options menu reveals all parameters that can be controlled with the computer keyboard by placing yellow arrows over them.

Figure 4.13

The number 1 key on the computer keyboard has been assigned to control the Pattern 1 button.

5. After you have assigned all eight Pattern buttons, deselect Keyboard Control Edit mode in the Options menu (the check mark will disappear), and then select Enable Keyboard Control from the Options menu.

6. Now you can select Patterns 1 through 8 by clicking numbers 1 through 8 on your computer keyboard!

If you wish to clear the mapping you have done, you can simply right-click (Ctrl-click, Mac) on the desired parameter and choose Clear Keyboard Control Mapping from the pop-up menu. It is not necessary to be in Keyboard Control Edit mode to do this, but it is helpful, since then you will be able to see all the mapping you have done simultaneously represented on your screen.

It is possible to assign Keyboard Control to a parameter without entering Keyboard Control Edit mode. This is done by right-clicking on the parameter (Ctrl-click, Mac) and selecting Edit Keyboard Control Mapping from the pop-up menu. However, you won't have the little arrows and numbers to help you keep track of what you've already mapped like you do in Keyboard Control Edit mode.

Instead, you will get a single dialog box for the parameter you are editing, which will allow you to see any previous mapping you have done for the parameter, as well as to learn a new control key by pressing a key on your computer keyboard (see Figure 4.14).

Figure 4.14

The Keyboard Control dialog box is launched by right-clicking on a parameter (Ctrl-click, Mac) and selecting Edit Keyboard Control Mapping from the pop-up menu. It is an alternative to using Keyboard Control Edit mode to create or change Keyboard Control assignments.

Although the examples in this chapter pertain to Redrum, all the Reason devices can be controlled with your computer keyboard using the preceding guidelines.

USE THE LATEST, GREATEST VERSION OF REASON!

When using Keyboard Control, it is especially important that you make sure you are using the latest version of Reason 3! Some versions previous to 3.04 may crash when using Keyboard Control. You can check your version by clicking on About Reason in the Help menu (Windows) or Reason menu (Mac). The latest version is available for registered users for download from www.propellerheads.se. Also, the latest version should generally run the most smoothly, contain the most bug fixes, and make the most efficient use of your CPU.

Selecting Patterns with Your MIDI Keyboard

The process for selecting patterns with your MIDI keyboard is similar to selecting them with your computer keyboard. Since the actual drum triggers are mapped to notes C1 through A1, the Mutes are mapped to C2 through E3, and the Solos are mapped to C4 through E5, let's map the Pattern buttons to A1 through A0, using only the white keys. This scenario only really works out well on an 88-key MIDI controller. Otherwise, you really won't have room for all this mapping on the same keyboard. A–1 through A0 is an easy span to grab, since A–1 is the very lowest note on an 88-key keyboard. Note that these keys will cease to transmit note values to other Reason instruments!

1. With Redrum in your Reason device rack, select Remote Override Edit mode from the Options menu. Click on Redrum to select it. This will highlight all parameters that can be controlled via MIDI (see Figure 4.15).

2. Double-click on the arrow over the Pattern 1 button. The arrow will turn into a twirling lightning bolt.

Figure 4.15
With Redrum selected in your Reason device rack, select Remote Override Edit mode from the Options menu. This will highlight all parameters that can be controlled via MIDI.

3. Press the A–1 key on your MIDI keyboard, and the lightning bolt will turn dark orange and stop spinning. If you mouse over it, a Tool Tip will tell you which note has been assigned (see Figure 4.16).

Figure 4.16
Mouse over a dark orange lightning bolt, and a Tool Tip will tell you which note has been assigned to control the parameter.

4. Repeat this process for the remaining seven Pattern buttons (using the B–1 key for Pattern 2, the C–key for Pattern 3, and so on). When you are done, all eight Pattern buttons should be assigned to notes A–1 through A0 on your MIDI keyboard.

5. After you have assigned all eight Pattern buttons, deselect Remote Override Edit mode in the Options menu.

6. Now you can select Patterns 1 through 8 by playing notes A–1 through A0 on your MIDI keyboard. If you like, you still have the B0 key left over for controlling the Pattern Enable button. You can assign its Remote Override Mapping the same way you did with the Pattern buttons.

If you wish to clear the mapping you have done, you can simply right-click (Ctrl-click, Mac) on the desired parameter and choose Clear Remote Override Mapping from the pop-up menu. It is not necessary to be in Remote Override Edit mode to do this, but it is helpful, since then you will be able to see all the mapping you have done simultaneously represented on your screen.

You can refer to this process when mapping any MIDI controller to any function in Reason that allows Remote Override Mapping. For additional details, please see your Reason operation manual. Now back to our regularly scheduled program: Making beats with Redrum!

Pattern Length/Edit Steps

Redrum allows you to create patterns of anywhere between one and 64 steps in length, though only a maximum of 16 steps can be shown on the Redrum interface at one time. If you desire, each pattern can be set to contain a different number of steps. The following settings determine the number of steps in a pattern and which of those steps are currently being displayed or edited.

- **Pattern Length**—The Pattern Length setting determines the number of steps that a pattern will play before repeating (see Figure 4.17). By default, the Pattern Length is set at 16 steps, which is the maximum that can be displayed or edited at one time (since there are 16 Step buttons). Decreasing this number will not delete any steps you had programmed beyond the new lower Pattern Length value. Those steps will still be there but simply will not be played (just like song data after the right locator when playback is looped). Patterns in odd meters can be created by adjusting the Pattern Length to values such as 5, 7, 9, 11, and so on. Pattern lengths in excess of 16 steps will require the use of the Edit Steps switch in order to edit the additional steps. The maximum pattern length is 64 steps. You can program different Pattern Length settings for each pattern within a single instance of Redrum.

- **Edit Steps**—When pattern lengths beyond 16 steps are used, the Edit Steps switch is used to view and edit the additional steps (see Figure 4.18). It can be switched between four groups of 16 steps. Of course, all steps specified by the Pattern Length value will play regardless of the position of the Edit Steps switch.

Figure 4.17

The Pattern Length setting determines the number of steps that a pattern will play before repeating.

Figure 4.18

The Edit Steps switch is used to choose which group of 16 steps you are editing in the pattern-based programmer.

123

Pattern Resolution

The length (or note value) of each step is determined by the Pattern Resolution setting (see Figure 4.19). The default is 1/16, meaning that each step is a 1/16 note. You can program different Pattern Resolution settings for each pattern within a single instance of Redrum. Although changing this setting while playing back a pattern will cause the pattern to play back more rapidly or more slowly, it has no effect on the Reason song tempo.

Figure 4.19

The Pattern Resolution knob is used to determine the length (or note value) of each step in your pattern.

Shuffle

When the Shuffle option is activated (see Figure 4.20), all 1/16 notes that fall between 1/8 notes are delayed to a degree determined by the Pattern Shuffle control on the far right of the Reason Transport Panel (see Figure 4.21). Adding shuffle gives your rhythms a swing feel. A couple of famous examples of shuffles used in rock/pop music are "Rosanna" by Toto and "Fool in the Rain" by Led Zeppelin. The following exercise should give you a feel for using the Shuffle option in your rhythms.

Figure 4.20

When the Shuffle option is activated, all 1/16 notes that fall between 1/8 notes are delayed to a degree determined by the Pattern Shuffle knob on the Reason Transport Panel.

Figure 4.21

The Pattern Shuffle control on the Reason Transport Panel determines the amount of shuffle (how much 1/16 notes that fall between 1/8 notes are delayed) for any Redrum (or Matrix) in the Reason rack on which the Shuffle button is activated.

1. Start with an empty rack. Create an instance of the reMix mixer, and then create an instance of Redrum.

2. Open Redrum's Patch Browser and select Reason Factory Sound Bank > Redrum Drum Kits > Heavy Kits > Dublab HeavyKit1.drp.

3. On Redrum, click the Channel 8 Select button.

4. Click on Step button 1, hold down your mouse button, and drag all the way across so that all 16 pads are activated. Then click on the Run button. You will hear the closed hi-hat playing a 1/16 note pattern.

5. Click the Shuffle button and hear the swing effect. Then in the Reason Transport Panel, experiment with the Pattern Shuffle knob. Turning it all the way to the left will result in no shuffle (no delay of 1/16 notes that fall in between 1/8 notes) and all the way to the right will result in a maximum delay of these 1/16 notes. Return the knob to 12 o'clock for a natural shuffle feel.

6. Click the Channel 4 Select button. Click Step buttons 5 and 13 so they light up and you hear the snare hit on these beats.

7. Click the Channel 1 Select button. Activate Step buttons 1, 6, 7, 8, 10, and 11 (see Figure 4.22). You will hear the kick drum play these beats.

8. You may notice that the hi-hat sounds oppressively robotic. To make it sound a bit more human, click the Channel 8 Select button. Put the Dynamic switch in the Soft position. Then click on the even-numbered Step buttons so that they turn yellow. Now the "ands" in "1 and 2 and 3 and 4..." will be softer, and the hi-hat pattern will sound a bit more natural. You can even try taking out the even-numbered hi-hat hits, and the kick drum will still carry the shuffle feel.

Figure 4.22
After clicking on the Channel 1 Select button, click on Step buttons 1, 6, 7, 8, 10, and 11, and you will hear the kick drum play these beats.

This exercise is saved as Shuffle Basics in the Redrum In Action folder on the CD-ROM. When playing back the pattern, you can deactivate the Shuffle button to hear the straight feel, and then reactivate Shuffle to hear the "swung" feel. Please note that Shuffle can be activated or deactivated individually for each pattern within a single instance of Redrum. The Pattern Shuffle knob on the Reason Transport Panel, however, is global and affects all shuffled patterns equally.

Pattern Functions

The following functions can either be selected from the Edit menu (when Redrum is highlighted) or from the context menu, which is the menu that pops up when you right-click (Ctrl-click, Mac) on Redrum.

- **Clear Pattern**—In addition to the self-explanatory Cut, Copy, and Paste Pattern commands, you also have the Clear Pattern command at your disposal. It will clear all data from the currently selected pattern so you can start fresh.

- **Shift Pattern Left**—Moves all the notes in the selected pattern one step to the left.

- **Shift Pattern Right**—Moves all the notes in the selected pattern one step to the right.

- **Shift Drum Left**—Moves all the notes for the selected drum channel one step to the left.

- **Shift Drum Right**—Moves all the notes for the selected drum channel one step to the right.

- **Randomize Pattern**—This awesome feature spontaneously generates a brand new completely random drum pattern.

- **Randomize Drum**—Generates a random pattern for the selected drum channel, leaving all the other drum channels unaffected. Great for snare drums and hand claps!

- **Alter Pattern**—Randomly rearranges the notes and velocities of an existing pattern. Unlike the Randomize function, the Alter Pattern function does not create something from nothing. If there is no pattern to rearrange, no notes will be played. It only rearranges existing values.

- **Alter Drum**—Does the same thing as Alter Pattern, but it only affects the currently selected drum channel, leaving all other drum channels unaffected.

- **Copy Pattern to Track**—Sends the currently selected pattern to a track on the Reason Sequencer, repeating the pattern as many times as is necessary to span the distance between the left and right locators. This allows more detailed editing of the pattern than can be done within Redrum itself. When controlling Redrum with the Sequencer, it is a good idea to disable the Pattern Section of Redrum.

Randomize It!

Redrum's Randomize functions have got to be my favorite part of working with Redrum. They are so cool we simply must play with them right now!

1. Start with an empty rack. Create an instance of the reMix mixer, and then create an instance of Redrum. Turn up the Song Tempo setting to 133 in the Reason Transport Panel.

2. Open Redrum's Patch Browser and select Reason Factory Sound Bank > Redrum Drum Kits > Electronic Kits > Electronic Kit 6.drp. Turn on High Quality Interpolation.

3. Turn up the bass drum volume by turning the Channel 1 Level knob up to 85 (about 2 o'clock).

4. Right-click on Redrum (Ctrl-click, Mac), and then select Randomize Pattern from the pop-up menu. Note that Randomize Pattern is also available in the Edit menu.

5. Click Run to hear the pattern.

6. Leave Channel 1 and Channel 2 panned at center, but use the Pan knobs to pan the other channels left and right to varying degrees (see Figure 4.23). You should have some nice stereo action going on now.

Figure 4.23
Leave Channel 1 and Channel 2 panned at center, but use the Pan knobs on the other channels to pan them left and right to varying degrees.

7. Select Pattern 2 by clicking the Pattern 2 button. Select Randomize Pattern again to create a brand new pattern.

8. From the Edit menu, select Copy Pattern. Click the Pattern 3 button, then select Paste Pattern from the Edit menu. Now Pattern 3 is identical to Pattern 2.

9. Click the Select button on Channel 1. This is the bass drum. Then move the Dynamic switch into the Hard position.

10. Click and drag across all 16 Step buttons so they are all white (inactive). You should not hear the kick drum any more.

11. Now click on Step buttons 1, 5, 9, and 13 so that you have a "four on the floor" bass drum pattern (see Figure 4.24).

12. From the Edit menu, select Copy Pattern. Click the Pattern 4 button, then select Paste Pattern from the Edit menu. Now Pattern 4 is identical to Pattern 3. Then with Channel 1 selected, click Step button 15. Now you can alternate between Patterns 3 and 4, going with Pattern 4 whenever you want that little pick-up note on the bass drum.

Figure 4.24
Click on Step buttons 1, 5, 9, and 13 so that you have a "four on the floor" bass drum pattern.

I have filled up all eight patterns in Pattern Bank A using the techniques above and saved the song as Random Electronic in the Redrum In Action folder on your CD-ROM. It should be obvious how quickly you can come up with some awesome electronic beats using these techniques. As you listen to the patterns you have created in the preceding exercise, please try loading other Redrum patches while the patterns play. Listen to the other Electronic Kits, Techno Kits, DrumNbass Kits, Glitch Kits, or anything that strikes your fancy. You will become familiar with the sounds of the different kits and with the radically different musical feels that can be produced by the same pattern played through different kits. Also keep in mind that once you find a kit you like, you can replace individual drums. I often find that almost every drum in a kit sounds great, but I need to try several different bass drums (usually Channel 1) before I find one that fits the song I'm working on.

Dynamic Switch

Redrum's Pattern section allows you to enter each step note with one of three velocity values: Soft, Medium, or Hard. This is achieved by setting the Dynamic switch to the desired setting before clicking on a Step button (see Figure 4.25). Although Redrum is capable of receiving any velocity value between 0 and 127 (from a MIDI controller or the Reason Sequencer), Redrum's pattern-based programmer is limited to these three velocities. Which of the three velocities has been chosen is indicated by the color of the Step button. Soft steps are yellow, Medium steps are orange, and Hard steps are red. The velocity setting of a step will only have an effect if the drum channel it triggers has Velocity to Level, Velocity to Tone, or Velocity to Pitch Bend values other than zero (see the "Redrum Channel Structure" section later in this chapter).

Figure 4.25

The Dynamic switch is used to determine which velocity value will be assigned when you click on a Step button.

Flam

When you double-strike a drum, this is known as a *flam*. In Redrum, applying flam to a step entry will add a second hit to the drum beat very soon after the first hit. The delay between these two hits is determined by the Flam knob (see Figure 4.26). The Flam knob is a global control, which will affect the amount of flam for all drums in all patterns to which flam is applied.

Figure 4.26

When flam has been applied to a Step button, the step will produce two drum hits instead of one. The Flam knob is used to set the amount of delay between these two hits.

Flam can be applied in two ways. First, you can click the Flam Edit button. It will light up red (see Figure 4.27). Any Step buttons you activate while the Flam Edit button is lit will have flam applied to them. For each step to which flam has been applied, the red LED above the Step button will be lit.

Figure 4.27

When the Flam Edit button is activated, it will light up red, and any Step buttons you activate will have flam applied to them.

The second way to apply flam does not require that the Flam Edit button be lit. You can simply click the little red LED above any Step button to apply flam to that step.

Flam can be used to accent certain notes and can also be used to create drum rolls. Both of these effects are covered in the following exercise.

1. Start with an empty rack. Create an instance of the reMix mixer, and then create an instance of Redrum.

2. Open Redrum's Patch Browser and select Reason Factory Sound Bank > Redrum Drum Kits > Tight Kits > Dublab TightKit1.drp.

3. Click the Channel 1 Select button. Then move the Dynamic switch into the Hard position. Now click on Step buttons 1, 5, 9, and 13 so that you have a "four on the floor" bass drum pattern. Click Run (if you have not already) to hear the pattern.

4. Click the Channel 8 Select button. This is a closed hi-hat. Move the Dynamic switch into the Medium position. Click on Step buttons 4, 8, 12, and 16.

5. Hey, wait a minute, that's not quite right! From the Edit menu, select Shift Drum Left. Now the hi-hats will be hitting on Steps 3, 7, 11, and 15, as they should.

6. Click the Channel 2 Select button. This is the snare drum. Activate Steps 8, 11, and 14, then move the Dynamic switch to the Soft position and activate Step 6.

7. Click directly above Step button 6 so that the LED lights up red and listen to the flam effect (see Figure 4.28).

Figure 4.28
Click directly above Step button 6 so that the LED lights up red to apply flam to Step 6 of the snare.

8. With the Dynamic switch set to Soft, click on Step buttons 1 and 2. Switch the Dynamic setting to Medium and click on Step button 3. Now switch the Dynamic setting to Hard and click on Step button 4.

9. Click above Steps 1 through 4 so that all four LEDs are lit up. You will hear flam applied to these four snare hits.

10. To create a roll, turn the Flam knob up to 3 o'clock. This will create more delay between the two hits on each step. The flam on Step 6 sounds kind of funny now, so you can deactivate it if you want by clicking the LED above the Step button switch. The LED should turn off, and the flam should disappear from that beat.

This exercise is saved as Flam Jam in the Redrum In Action folder on your CD-ROM. I apologize for the painfully corny name. By the way, with Channel 2 selected, this is a good time to experiment with applying Randomize Drum and Alter Drum to the snare. To maintain the kick and hi-hat pattern, you can use Copy Pattern, select an empty pattern, and then click Paste Pattern. You can randomize or alter the snare patterns this way until you fill up a pattern bank. Then if you switch between patterns while Redrum is playing, it will sound almost like you have a live drummer improvising on the snare drum. Of course, you can apply this knowledge to much more imaginative and grooving patterns than the simple kick and hi-hat pattern I created for the exercise!

Redrum Channel Structure

Unlike the reMix 14:12 mixer, which has 12 identical channel strips, in Redrum there are some different features included, depending on which of its 10 channels you are using. Before we focus on the differences, however, let's take a look at what each channel has in common.

Channel Select

Each Redrum channel has a Select button at the bottom of it (see Figure 4.29). This is used for selecting the channel for step programming. When you click the Select button on any channel, any steps that have been programmed for the drum on that channel will be indicated by the appropriate Step buttons lighting up. At any time during your pattern programming, you can click the Select button for any channel and add or remove steps (by clicking on the desired Step button), change velocity of certain notes using the Dynamic switch, or apply flam to any beat you like by clicking the little red LED directly above the desired Step button.

In addition to Channel Select, the following controls are also included in the same order on every channel of Redrum.

Figure 4.29

Each Redrum channel has a Select button at the bottom, which is used for selecting the channel for editing in the pattern-based programmer.

Mute and Solo

The Mute and Solo buttons at the top of each Redrum channel work the same way as the Mute and Solo buttons on any audio mixer (see Figure 4.30). Engaging the Mute on any channel stops audio output from that channel. Engaging the Solo on any channel mutes all other channels except for the soloed channel(s). Solo can be especially useful for isolating one drum to hear the part it is playing, tune it, or adjust its tone or other parameters. Mutes can be very effective for bringing drums in and out of the mix or making a drum mix minimal for a while, and then dramatically bringing the bass drum back in with the full mix. Just like anything else in Reason, the Mutes and Solos can be automated by recording a Redrum automation track in the Reason Sequencer. It's just a regular Sequencer track routed to Redrum, but instead of recording note info, you just mute and solo as needed while Reason is recording. Then when you play back, the Mutes and Solos will play back as you recorded them. You can keep going back and overdubbing, adding what you need until all your Mutes and Solos are in place.

Figure 4.30
The Mute and Solo buttons at the top of each Redrum channel
work the same way as the Mute and Solo buttons on any audio mixer.

Live performance is another matter, since it is impossible to click on two Mute buttons at once with your mouse! There is no Mute Group or Solo Group feature on Redrum (as you might find in a large professional mixing console). Propellerhead does have an answer to this issue. The Mutes and Solos are mapped to specific keys on your MIDI keyboard. To make it extra easy, they only used the white keys. There are 10 Mutes and 10 Solos, so if you use all your fingers and toes, you'll have it covered!

- The Mutes are mapped sequentially (starting at Channel 1 Mute) on the 10 white keys spanning C2 to E3.

- The Solos are mapped sequentially (starting at Channel 1 Solo) on the 10 white keys spanning C4 to E5.

Note that Mutes and Solos behave differently when controlled with a MIDI keyboard than they do when you use a mouse. When you click on a Mute or Solo button with your mouse, it remains muted or soloed until you click the button a second time (this is sometimes referred to as "toggle" behavior). However, when you control the Mutes and Solos with a MIDI keyboard, channels will only be muted or soloed as long as you are holding down the applicable keys on the keyboard. As soon as you let go, the affected Mute or Solo will immediately disengage. If Reason is in Record mode while you mute and solo with a MIDI keyboard and your Redrum Sequencer track is selected, the Mute and Solo automation information will still be recorded the same as if you had used the mouse to click the Mute and Solo buttons.

Effect Sends (S1 and S2)

Redrum's Effect Sends are especially useful when you are connecting Redrum to the reMix mixer on one stereo channel, instead of routing each individual drum to a separate channel on reMix (see Figure 4.31). On reMix (as well as on the smaller Micromix Line Mixer), each channel has its own Effect Sends. But when Redrum is connected to only one stereo channel of a mixer, using one or more Effect Sends (Aux Sends) on the mixer channel would apply the effects to all the drums simultaneously. Using Redrum's own Effect Sends allow you to send the audio signal from each individual drum to up to two separate effects at any level you want. If reMix is present at the top of the Reason device rack, when a new Redrum is created, Redrum's Send Out 1 and 2 (S1 and S2) outputs will be automatically routed to the first two available Chaining Aux inputs in the rear of reMix (see Figure 4.32). These inputs bypass the red Auxiliary Send Level knobs on the front of reMix, and send the signal directly to the effects device with no attenuation. Let's give this a spin and try out an odd meter while we're at it.

Figure 4.31

Redrum's Effect Sends are especially useful when you are connecting Redrum to the reMix mixer on one stereo channel, instead of routing each individual drum to a separate channel on reMix.

Figure 4.32

When a new Redrum is created, its Send Out 1 and 2 (S1 and S2) outputs will be automatically routed to the first two available Chaining Aux inputs in the rear of reMix.

1. Start with an empty rack. Create an instance of the reMix mixer, followed by an RV7000 Advanced Reverb and a DDL-1 Digital Delay. The effects will already be routed with the RV7000 on Effects Return 1 and the DDL-1 on Effects Return 2 (see Figure 4.33).

2. Create an instance of Redrum. Flip your rack around (using the Tab key on your computer keyboard), and you will see that Send Outs 1 and 2 of Redrum have been automatically routed to Chaining Aux inputs 1 and 2 of reMix. This means that the signal from Redrum's Send 1 will be processed by the RV7000 Reverb, and the signal from Redrum's Send 2 will be processed by the DDL-1 Digital Delay.

Figure 4.33
Create an instance of the reMix Mixer, followed by an RV7000 Advanced Reverb and a DDL-1 Digital Delay.
The effects will already be routed with the RV7000 on Effects Return 1 and the DDL-1 on Effects Return 2.

3. Flip the Reason device rack back around facing front. Open Redrum's Patch Browser, and select Reason Factory Sound Bank > Redrum Drum Kits > Tight Kits > Dublab TightKit1.drp.

4. Redrum does not react any differently, regardless of the time signature setting in the Reason Transport Panel; but for ease in editing, looping, and creating any additional tracks in the Reason Sequencer, let's set the time signature to 9/8, which will match what we are going to do in Redrum (see Figure 4.34). Leave the Click off for now, though.

Figure 4.34
The time signature should be set to 9/8 in the Reason Transport Panel.

5. On Redrum, set the number of Steps to 9, then set the Resolution to 1/8. Click the Run button.

6. Click the Channel 1 Select button, then move the Dynamic switch into the Hard position. Now click on Step buttons 1, 5, and 6 to place bass drum hits on those beats.

7. Click the Channel 2 Select button, and click on Step buttons 3 and 8 to place snare drum hits on those beats.

133

8. Click the Channel 8 Select button, then move the Dynamic switch into the Medium position. Click and drag your mouse across Step buttons 1 though 9 so that all nine steps are active.

9. Turn the Channel 2 Send 1 knob up to 10 o'clock. You should hear reverb applied to the snare drum. Now turn the Channel 2 Send 2 knob up to 12 o'clock. You will hear delay applied to the snare drum in such a way as to suggest grace notes being played on the snare drum (see Figure 4.35).

Figure 4.35
Turn up both Effect Send knobs on Channel 2 to apply reverb and delay to the snare drum. The little red light in between the Send knobs indicates that the sample being used for the snare drum is a stereo sample.

10. Turn the Channel 1 Send 2 knob up to 12 o'clock. You will hear delay applied to the kick drum.

11. Turn the Channel 8 Send 2 knob up to 12 o'clock. You will hear delay applied to the hi-hat.

I have saved this exercise as Nine with Effects in the Redrum In Action folder on your CD-ROM. Remember that if you would like to hear the pattern play without any effects, click the Solo button on Channel 1 of reMix.

Pan, Level, and Velocity to Level

The Pan knob included on each channel determines the selected drum's position in the stereo image. Pan settings are very important for creating a realistic-sounding acoustic kit, as well as for creating ear-catching electronic kits. The little red LED above the Pan knob (in between the Send knobs) lights up to indicate when a stereo sample is being used (see Figure 4.36). Its little label looks like an infinity symbol or a bipolar microphone pattern, but, of course, signifies stereo in this case. When it is not lit, this means a mono sample is being used, and the Pan knob will simply move the mono sample to the left or right of the stereo image. If the Stereo Sample LED is lit to indicate that a stereo sample is being used, then the Pan knob becomes a stereo balance control, emphasizing the left or right channel of the stereo sample.

Figure 4.36
The little red LED above the Pan knob (in between the Send knobs) lights up to indicate when a stereo sample is being used.

The Level knob, of course, controls the volume for the channel. The Velocity to Level knob (Vel, to the right of the Level knob) is used to determine to what degree velocity affects the volume level of the channel (see Figure 4.37). This is a bipolar control. If the Velocity to Level knob is set at 12 o'clock, then it will not matter what velocity you play on your MIDI controller, or what position Redrum's Velocity switch is set to; any note played on that channel will product the same volume level. Turning the Velocity to Level knob (Vel) to the right means that higher velocities will result in louder volume. Turning the knob to the left means that higher velocities will result in softer volume levels.

Figure 4.37
The Level knob controls the volume for the channel, while the Velocity to Level knob (Vel) is used to determine to what degree velocity affects the volume level of the channel.

Length Knob and Decay/Gate Switch

The Length knob is used to set the duration of the drum sound. The manner in which it does this is determined by the position of the Decay/Gate switch (see Figure 4.38).

Figure 4.38
The Length knob is used to set the duration of the drum sound. The manner in which it does this is determined by the position of the Decay/Gate switch.

- **Decay Mode (switch down)**—In this mode, the sound decays (or fades out) at a rate determined by the Length knob. If you are playing the sound from the Reason Sequencer, a MIDI controller, or a CV/Gate device (instead of using the Step buttons and Pattern section of Redrum), it won't matter how long you hold a note; once the note has been played, the sound will go through its entire decay cycle. This is the standard operation common to most drum machines.

- **Gate Mode (switch up)**—In this mode, there is no decay. When played with Redrum's Step buttons and Pattern section, the sound will play for a duration set by the Length knob, and then cut off. If you are playing the sound from the Reason Sequencer, a MIDI controller, or a CV/Gate device (instead of using the Step buttons and Pattern section of Redrum), the sound will either cut off after the time determined by the Length knob or when the note ends, whichever comes first. This can be very handy if you are using Redrum to play non-drum samples (such as sound effects), where it is important to play the whole sample or where you wish to control the cutoff point for the sample. It is also ideal for creating "gated" drum sounds (first made popular in the 1980s), where the tail of the drum sound is cut off abruptly.

The rest of the controls in this channel section vary depending on which channel you are using.

> ### IN GATE MODE, LOOPS MAY DRIVE YOU LOOPY
>
> Although Redrum is usually used for drum samples, it can load any Wave or AIFF file you like. Some of these samples may contain loops (as described in Chapter 3, "NN-XT" and Appendix A on the CD-ROM, entitled "NN-19"). When using the Redrum Pattern section, if the sample you have loaded contains a loop, and the Length knob is all the way up while you are in Gate mode, the sound will have infinite sustain (and actually infinite release) once played. That means once you trigger it, it will never shut up, even after you turn off the Run button. (It's not a bug, it's a feature!) This problem is easily solved by turning down the Length knob a bit. Also, although this behavior manifests when clicking the Run button to stop Redrum pattern playback, clicking the Stop button on the Reason Transport Panel stops all the samples from playing.

Pitch and Pitch Bend

All Redrum channels have a Pitch knob, which can tune the sample within a range of plus or minus one octave. In the case of channels 1–5 and 8–10, that's the end of the story as it relates to Pitch control (see Figure 4.39). On all channels, the Pitch knob has a little red LED above it, which turns on whenever the pitch is set to any value other than zero (meaning that the sample is no longer playing back at its original pitch).

Figure 4.39

All Redrum channels have a Pitch knob, which can tune the sample within a range of plus or minus one octave.

Channels 6 and 7 have some extra control over pitch via the following three controls (see Figure 4.40):

Figure 4.40

Channels 6 and 7 have some extra control over pitch thanks to the addition of Pitch Bend, Pitch Bend Rate, and Velocity to Pitch Bend controls.

■ **Pitch Bend (Bend)**—This Pitch Bend knob determines the pitch at which the sound will start before bending back to the main Pitch value (the value at which the Pitch knob is set). Positive Pitch Bend values will cause the note to start at a higher pitch, and then bend down to the Pitch value set by the Pitch knob, while negative Pitch Bend values will cause the note to start at a lower pitch and then bend up to the Pitch value set by the Pitch knob.

■ **Pitch Bend Rate (Rate)**—The Pitch Bend Rate knob controls the speed at which the sound will bend up or down. It is similar to Portamento in that the higher the value of the Pitch Bend Rate knob, the slower the bend.

■ **Velocity to Pitch Bend (Vel)**—The Velocity to Pitch Bend knob determines how velocity will affect Pitch Bend. Positive values will result in higher velocities causing higher starting pitches, while negative values will result in higher velocities causing lower starting pitches.

All of the Pitch controls (including Bend, Rate, and Vel) have red LED indicators to show when the controls are active (meaning a value other than zero has been selected).

1. Start with an empty rack. Create an instance of the reMix mixer, and then create an instance of Redrum.

2. Open the Channel 6 Sample Browser and browse to the NN-19 Samples folder on your CD-ROM. In the Prepared Bowls folder, choose Bowl F#1.wav.

3. Play the F1 key on your MIDI keyboard (MIDI note number 41 if you are playing pads).

4. Turn the Channel 6 Pitch Bend knob to a value of −40 (about 9 o'clock). Now play the F1 key, and you will hear the note start lower and bend up to the original pitch (see Figure 4.41).

Figure 4.41
Turn the Channel 6 Pitch Bend knob to a value of −40 (about 9 o'clock).

5. Now turn the Channel 6 Pitch Bend knob to a value of +40 (about 3 o'clock). Play the F1 key again, and you will hear the note start higher and then bend down to the original pitch.

6. Experiment with the Pitch knob. The note will always bend to whatever value is set by the Pitch knob. When you are done playing with the Pitch knob, return it to its center position. The Pitch Bend knob should still be at a position of 3 o'clock.

7. By default, the Rate knob is set at 12 o'clock. Turn it up to 3 o'clock and trigger the sample again. You will hear a much longer bend. Then gradually turn the Rate knob to the left, while triggering the sample over and over again. Eventually, the bend will happen so fast that you will not be able to detect it. When you are done experimenting with the Rate knob, return it to its center position.

8. Turn the Pitch Bend knob back to its center position. Now there will be no bend when you strike a key.

9. Turn Channel 6 Velocity to Pitch Bend knob all the way to the right (its maximum positive value). Play the F1 key with varying degrees of velocity, and you will find that the harder you strike it, the higher the pitch will be at the start of the sound before it bends back down to the original pitch (see Figure 4.42).

137

10. Now turn the Channel 6 Velocity to Pitch Bend knob all the way to the left (its maximum negative value). Play the F1 key with varying degrees of velocity, and you will find that the harder you strike it, the lower the pitch will be at the start of the sound before it bends back up to the original pitch.

Figure 4.42

With the Velocity to Pitch Bend knob turned all the way to the right, the harder the note is played, the higher the pitch will be at the start of the sound before it bends back down to the original pitch.

Tone

Channels 1, 2, and 10 each have a Tone knob, accompanied by a Velocity to Tone knob (see Figure 4.43). Turning the Tone knob to the right makes the sound brighter by boosting the high frequencies. The center position has no effect. Turning the knob to the left rolls off highs making the sound darker. The Velocity to Tone knob is a very cool feature that can make drums sound more lifelike. When the knob is turned right of center, higher velocities will result in brighter sounds. This mimics real life, where striking a drum harder (or piano key, for that matter) results not only in a louder sound, but also in a brighter sound. To make sounds louder in response to higher velocities, you use the Velocity to Level knob (with a positive setting). To make sound brighter in response to higher velocities, you use the Velocity to Tone knob (with a positive value). Of course, negative values will have an inverse effect, with higher velocities producing a darker tone. The following exercise uses a positive value for Velocity to Tone, so the harder you play, the brighter the sound will be. This should add realism to the snare drum sample used in the exercise.

Figure 4.43

Channels 1, 2, and 10 each have a Tone knob, accompanied by a Velocity to Tone knob.

1. Start with an empty rack. Create an instance of the reMix mixer and then create an instance of Redrum.

2. Open Redrum's Patch Browser and select Reason Factory Sound Bank > Redrum Drum Kits > Heavy Kits > Dublab HeavyKit1.drp.

3. Play the C#1 key on your MIDI keyboard (MIDI note number 37 if you are playing pads). This will trigger the snare drum on Channel 2. Play with varying degrees of velocity. The volume of the sound will change depending on the velocity, but the tonal characteristics will remain the same.

4. Turn the Channel 2 Tone knob all the way to the left (all the way down) and turn the Channel 2 Velocity to Tone (Vel) knob to the right up to a value of +30 (see Figure 4.44).

5. Strike the C#1 key (MIDI note 37) again with varying degrees of velocity. The harder you play, the brighter the drum will sound.

Figure 4.44

Turn the Channel 2 Tone knob all the way to the left (all the way down), and turn the Channel 2 Velocity to Tone (Vel) knob to the right up to a value of +30.

I have saved this exercise as Velocity to Tone in the Redrum In Action folder on your CD-ROM.

Sample Start

Channels 3, 4, 5, 8, and 9 have a Sample Start knob accompanied by a Velocity to Sample Start knob (see Figure 4.45). Redrum's Sample Start works the same way as the Sample Start knob on the front of the NN-19. Its default setting of zero (all the way to the left) means that the sample starts at the beginning. The farther to the right you turn the knob, the farther along into the sample the start point will move. So if you had a sample of yourself counting 1-2-3-4, the sample would start on "1" if the Sample Start is set on zero (all the way to the left). As you turn the knob to the right, you will hear the sample start on "2," then eventually "3," then "4" (and points in between).

Figure 4.45

Channels 3, 4, 5, 8, and 9 have a Sample Start knob accompanied by a Velocity to Sample Start knob.

Velocity to Sample Start is a bipolar control. Positive values will result in higher velocities, starting the sound farther along into the sample (moving the Sample Start value forward). Negative values will only have an effect if the Sample Start knob is set at a value greater than zero. This is because it is impossible to start playback *before* the beginning of the sample.

Using negative values for Velocity to Sample Start can add realism to certain drum sounds. This way, the very first (and often sharpest) transients in the attack of the drum sound will only be heard when you hit the very hard notes. The following exercise will illustrate this.

1. Start with an empty rack. Create an instance of the reMix mixer and then create an instance of Redrum.

2. Open Redrum's Patch Browser and select Reason Factory Sound Bank > Redrum Drum Kits > Heavy Kits > Dublab HeavyKit1.drp.

3. Play the E1 key on your MIDI keyboard (MIDI note number 40 if you are playing pads). This will trigger the tom-tom on Channel 5. Play with varying degrees of velocity. The volume of the sound will change depending on the velocity, but the tonal characteristics will remain the same.

4. Turn the Channel 5 Sample Start knob up to 12 o'clock, and turn the Velocity to Sample Start knob (Vel) down to 9 o'clock (a value of about −40; see Figure 4.46).

5. Strike the E1 key (MIDI note 40) again with varying degrees of velocity. You will not hear the sharp attack at the start of the sample when you play softly, but that sharp attack will come in when you play hard.

Figure 4.46
Turn the Sample Start knob up to 12 o'clock, and turn the Velocity to Sample Start knob (Vel) down to 9 o'clock (a value of about −40).

I have saved the above exercise as Negative Velocity to Start in the Redrum In Action folder on your CD-ROM.

Global Settings

The following settings affect multiple Redrum channels. The Channel 8&9 Exclusive option only applies to channels 8 and 9, but Propellerhead still refers to it as a global setting. High Quality Interpolation and Master Level affect all Redrum channels.

High Quality Interpolation and Master Level

By now you should be familiar with the concept of High Quality Interpolation (see Figure 4.47). When it is activated, a more advanced interpolation algorithm is used to calculate sample playback. This results in higher fidelity, especially when playing samples containing a lot of high frequency content. It uses a few more CPU cycles to do this, but the performance hit is negligible. Since we want everything to sound as good as possible all the time, I am in favor of always using High Quality Interpolation.

Figure 4.47
Engage High Quality Interpolation for higher fidelity, especially when playing samples containing a lot of high frequency content.

Every Reason Instrument (except for the Combinator) has a master volume control on it somewhere, and Redrum's Master Level control is located in the top-left corner (see Figure 4.48).

In case you missed it, that's where it is. There is not much more to say about it. Turn it to the left, and the sound gets quieter. Turn it to the right, and the sound gets louder.

Figure 4.48
Redrum's Master Level control is located in the top-left corner of the Redrum interface.

Channel 8&9 Exclusive

When the Channel 8&9 Exclusive button is activated, the sounds on Channels 8 and 9 will be exclusive of each other, meaning that when a sound is triggered on Channel 8, it will be cut off as soon as a sound is played on Channel 9, and vice versa (see Figure 4.49). This is handy for adding realism to hi-hats, where a closed hi-hat is loaded into one channel and an open hi-hat is loaded into the other channel. To get a feel for this, please try the following exercise.

Figure 4.49
With the Channel 8&9 Exclusive button activated, a sound triggered on Channel 8 will be cut off as soon as a sound is played on Channel 9, and vice versa.

1. Start with an empty rack. Create an instance of the reMix mixer, and then create an instance of Redrum.

2. Open Redrum's Patch Browser and select Reason Factory Sound Bank > Redrum Drum Kits > Tight Kits > Dublab TightKit1.drp.

3. Click the Channel 8 Select button. This is a closed hi-hat. Click and drag your mouse across all 16 Step buttons so that they are all lit up yellow, then click on Steps 1, 5, 9, and 13 to deactivate them.

4. Click the Channel 9 Select button. This is the open hi-hat. Click on Steps 1, 5, 9, and 13 so that they are lit up yellow.

5. Click the Run button. Now practice turning the Channel 8&9 Exclusive button on and off. When it is on, the open hi-hat will cease to ring out as soon as the closed hi-hat is played. If the Channel 8&9 Exclusive button is off, the open hi-hat will continue to ring out even when the closed hi-hat is played, which would be physically impossible for a real hi-hat!

This is a super simple exercise, but I saved it for you anyway as Channel 8_9 Exclusive in the Redrum In Action folder on your CD-ROM.

Redrum and the Reason Sequencer

Using the Reason Sequencer can add a whole new level of flexibility when it comes to editing your beats. If you have already created a pattern in Redrum's Pattern section and would like to edit it in the Reason Sequencer, you will use the Copy Pattern to Track option.

1. Start with an empty rack. Create an instance of the reMix mixer, and then create an instance of Redrum.

2. Load any kit you like into Redrum. We are going to use the Randomize Pattern feature, so you may wish to use some kind of electronic kit.

3. Right-click on Redrum (Ctrl-click, Mac), and then select Randomize Pattern from the pop-up menu. Remember that Randomize Pattern is also available in the Edit menu.

4. Click on the magnifying glass at the bottom of the Reason Sequencer until the zoom is so large you can only see bars 1, 2, and3. Set the right locator on bar 2 and leave the left locator set on bar 1.

5. Right-click on Redrum (Ctrl-click, Mac), and then select Copy Pattern to Track from the pop-up menu. Copy Pattern to Track is also available in the Edit menu. The MIDI data for your pattern will appear between the left and right locators in the Reason Sequencer.

6. Turn off the Enable Pattern Section button on Redrum and then press Play in the Reason Transport Panel to hear the beat.

7. Click on the Switch to Arrange Mode button, and you will see the Drum Lane, which is what you will use to edit the MIDI notes in the pattern. You may actually have to drag the top of the Sequencer window up until you can see the Drum Lane. Notice that rather than a piano keyboard, each of the 10 drum channels is listed (see Figure 4.50).

Once the pattern is copied to the Reason Sequencer, you can requantize it (including Groove Quantize), do fine adjustments to velocity, and easily rearrange the notes in the pattern.

If you like, you can eschew the pattern-based programmer altogether and simply use the Reason Sequencer from the beginning. Although you can draw in the notes with the Pencil tool, you can get some very lifelike results playing in the notes with a MIDI controller. If you are playing a MIDI keyboard, it is useful to know that Redrum Channels 1 through 10 are mapped to notes C1 through

A1 on your MIDI keyboard. It is also useful to know that this translates to MIDI note numbers 36 through 45, especially if you are playing a MIDI percussion controller with pads that can be assigned using MIDI note number values.

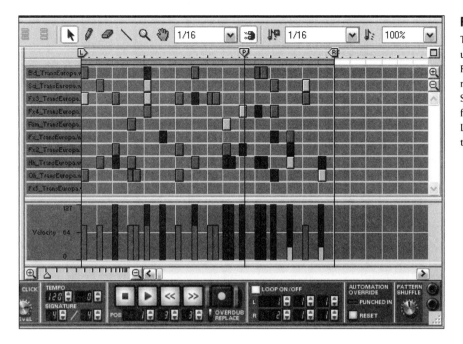

Figure 4.50

The Drum Lane is used for editing Redrum MIDI information in the Reason Sequencer. In this figure, the Velocity Lane is shown below the Drum Lane.

Redrum Automation

Just about any parameter in Reason can be automated if you move or change it while you are recording on the track routed to the device you are adjusting. Redrum is no exception, and automating Mutes and pattern changes are probably the two forms of Redrum automation you will do the most. Let's give it a run-through.

1. Open the Reason song called Random Electronic found in the Redrum In Action folder on your CD-ROM.

2. Mute Channels 1 through 7 (see Figure 4.51). You may want to turn on the Click in the Reason Transport Panel to help you keep time in this exercise.

3. Select Pattern 3. Click Record, and then click Play in the Reason Transport Panel.

4. Starting with Channel 7, every bar or two (on the beat), unmute the next channel to the left until all Channels are unmuted.

5. Now practice switching back and forth between Pattern 3 and Pattern 4. The only difference between the two patterns is the extra bass drum hit at the end of Pattern 4. If you like, you can practice switching among the other patterns as well.

143

Figure 4.51

Mute Redrum
Channels 1
through 7.

6. Now mute Channels 1 through 7, one by one, from left to right (on the beat). When all seven channels are muted, click the Pattern button. This will not stop playback of the Reason song, but it will stop the pattern from playing any more.

7. Click Stop on the Reason Transport Panel. Notice the green outlines around everything you automated. Click Stop again so that the Song Position marker (labled P) goes back to the start of the song.

8. Click Play on the Reason Transport, and you will see your Mutes and pattern changes happen like magic!

I have saved this exercise with the name Automaton in the Redrum In Action folder on your CD-ROM.

Redrum Rear Panel Routing

Earlier in this chapter, you were introduced to the rear panel of Redrum in order to become acquainted with the function of the Effect Sends. Now please flip your Reason rack around and check out of Redrum's rear panel (see Figure 4.52).

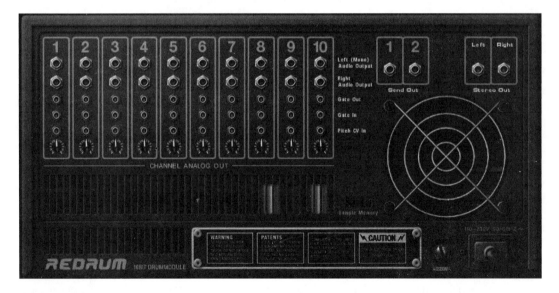

Figure 4.52

Redrum's rear panel.

■ **Audio Outputs**—Each Redrum channel has its own individual audio outputs (see Figure 4.52). This allows you to route each drum to a separate channel in the reMix 14:12 mixer, thus giving you the opportunity to send individual Redrum channel outputs through insert effects (such as compressors or EQs). You can also use the EQ on the individual reMix channels to custom EQ each drum, as well as apply any of reMix's four Auxiliary Send/Returns individually to each drum. For mono drum samples, you should use the Left (Mono) output on the Redrum channel. You will then use the Pan control on reMix to control the drum's position in the stereo image. When using stereo samples, you can connect the left and right outputs of the Redrum channel to the left and right inputs of a single reMix channel (see Figure 4.53). Note that when you use an individual Redrum Channel output for a sound, that sound will be automatically excluded from Redrum's master Stereo Out.

Figure 4.53

When using stereo samples, you can connect the left and right outputs of the Redrum channel to the left and right inputs of a single reMix channel. In this figure, Channel 10 of Redrum is using a stereo sample and has its left and right outputs connected to the left and right inputs of reMix Channel 10.

■ **Gate Out**—Sends out a gate signal each time a drum sound is played, whether the drum sound is triggered from a pattern, via MIDI or by using the Trigger button at the top of the Redrum channel. In this way you can use the Redrum as a "trig sequencer," controlling other devices with CV Gate inputs. The duration of the gate signal will depend on the Decay/Gate setting for the sound. In Decay mode, a short "trig pulse" is sent out, regardless of the position of that channel's Length knob. In Gate mode, the length of the gate signal will be the same as the same length as the drum note. When drums are triggered by Redrum's Pattern section, this length is determined by the setting of the Length knob on that Redrum channel.

145

- **Gate In**—The Gate input allows you to trigger the sound with the output from another CV/Gate device.

- **Pitch CV In**—Allows you to control the pitch of the drum sound with control voltage from another CV device.

- **Send Out 1–2**—These are the Effect Send outputs for the Send signals controlled with the S1 and S2 knobs at the top of each Redrum channel, as described in the "Redrum Channel Structure" portion of this chapter.

- **Stereo Out**—This is Redrum's master stereo output, which outputs a stereo mix of all your drum sounds, except those for which you have used individual channel outputs.

- **Sample Memory Display Window**—This display tells you how much space (in megabytes) the sounds you have loaded into Redrum are taking up in RAM.

Now that you have become familiar with Redrum, it's time to bring it all together with the last stop on our tour of Reason's virtual instruments: the Combinator!

5 The Combinator

First included in Reason 3.0, the Combinator is one of the most powerful tools in your Reason rack (see Figure 5.1). It is also straightforward and easy to use. It allows you to create any kind of setup you can imagine, containing any combination of effects and instruments, and save them as one instantly recallable patch. Now you can control as many Reason synths as your computer can handle, all at the same time and on one Sequencer track. If you want, you can play one chord on your keyboard and hear a virtual wall of Malströms and Subtractors spring into action. You can set up velocity ranges and key ranges so that the keys you play or how hard you play them determines which synths will be triggered. For me, the Combinator alone is worth moving from Reason 2.5 to Reason 3.

Figure 5.1
The Combinator turns Reason into a powerful instrument creation toolkit!

Combinator Patches

The Reason Factory Sound Bank includes numerous Combinator presets, which are called *Combis*, and have the .cmb file extension. Becoming familiar with these presets is a great way to get some inspiration and direction in creating your own Combi patches. Note that any Combis in the Factory Sound Bank with [Run] at the end of their name contain a pattern device (Redrum or Matrix).

Combi patches are divided into two basic types:

- **Effect**—As you might guess, effect Combis are used to process sound, and do not contain any instruments with which to generate sound. The MClass Mastering Suite Combi, which is selectable from the Create menu, is an effect Combi. Since this book is focused on the Reason instruments, I will not be discussing effect Combis in much detail.

- **Instrument**—These include sound-generating instrument devices, such as Subtractor, NN-XT, or Redrum, and can also contain effect devices. The only limits to the fatness of layered sounds that can be created in this way would be what your computer and your brain can handle!

Now let's get acquainted with the Combinator itself.

The Combinator's Top (Narrow) Panel

Open a new document and create a Combinator. Take a look at the topmost panel (the narrow panel that still shows when the Combinator is folded) and note that, in addition to the usual Select/Browse/Save patch buttons, there is also a Bypass/On/Off switch like that found on Reason effect devices (see Figure 5.2). Also included are Input and Output level meters, a MIDI Note On indicator, and an External Routing indicator, which will light up if you route audio or modulation output directly from any Combinator device to another device outside of the Combinator. The External Routing indicator (see Figure 5.3) can be considered a warning indicator because it alerts you to the presence of external connections, which will not be saved with the Combi patch.

Figure 5.2
The narrow panel at the top of the Combinator can display quite a bit of information.

Figure 5.3
The External Routing indicator alerts you to the presence of external connections, which will not be saved with the Combi patch.

The Controller Panel

The Combinator's Controller Panel is visible whenever the Combinator is unfolded (see Figure 5.4). It consists of the elements in the following list.

Figure 5.4

The Combinator's Controller Panel.

- **Pitch**—Sends pitch bend info to all instrument devices contained in a Combi. Bend range is set individually in each instrument device's Range field.

- **Mod Wheel**—The Mod wheel sends modulation data to all instrument devices contained in a Combi. The effect of this modulation data is determined by the individual Mod wheel assignments made within each instrument device.

- **Run Pattern Devices**—Starts or stops all pattern devices in a Combi. This button is automatically activated when you press Play on the Transport Panel.

- **Bypass All FX**—Bypasses all effects devices included in a Combi, switching all insert effects to Bypass mode and switching off all effects connected as send effects to a mixer device. Effects already bypassed or turned off will not be affected by this button.

- **Show Programmer**—Shows or hides the Programmer Panel.

- **Show Devices**—Shows or hides all devices included in a Combi.

- **Rotary Knobs**—Can be assigned to control parameters in any devices included in a Combi. Rotary knob control assignments are made in the Modulation Routing section of the Programmer Panel. Rotary knob labels can be customized by clicking on the label and typing in a name.

- **Button Controls**—Can be assigned to control any button-controlled parameters in devices included in a Combi. Note that the Button controls only switch between two values, so if the device parameter you are controlling has more than two possible values (like an On/Off/Bypass switch or an LFO Waveform button), a Combinator Button control will only toggle between two of those values. As with the Rotary knobs, you can assign useful names to your Button controls by clicking on the labels and typing away.

The Programmer

Click the Show Programmer button and check out the Programmer Panel (the pretty blue screen), which is really the nerve center of your Combinator. The Programmer is not at all difficult to master (see Figure 5.5). In fact, if you have already mastered the NN-XT, this should be a walk in the park. The Programmer can be divided into the following areas of functionality.

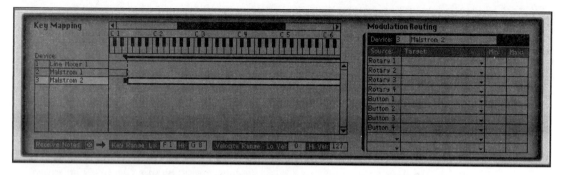

Figure 5.5

The Programmer is where you assign key ranges, velocity ranges, and modulation routing within the Combinator.

Device Area

The Device area is where all the Reason devices included in the Combi are listed and can be selected for editing (see Figure 5.6). They appear, from top to bottom, in the order in which they are inserted in the Combinator. You can click on one device at a time to select it for editing.

Figure 5.6

The Device area is where you select which device is to be edited in the Programmer.

Directly below the Device area is the Receive Notes parameter. This is activated by clicking in the Receive Notes checkbox. It can only be activated for instruments and for the BV12 Vocoder. This must be active in order for the selected device to receive MIDI note information.

Key Mapping Section

The Key Mapping section is where you assign key and velocity ranges to the instruments included in a Combinator (see Figure 5.7). The Key Mapping section includes the following areas, which are similar to those of the NN-XT.

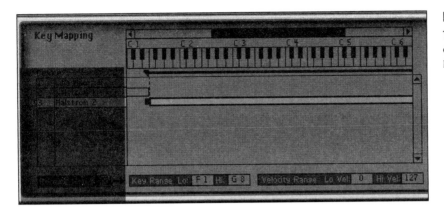

Figure 5.7
The Key Mapping section
of the Combinator's
Programmer Panel.

- **Keyboard Area**—In addition to providing a visual reference for mapping key ranges, the Keyboard area can be used for auditioning sounds by Alt-clicking on the desired keys (see Figure 5.8). This will turn your cursor into a little speaker icon, and all instruments in the Combi set to Receive Notes will be triggered, regardless of which device is selected in the Device area of the combinatory Programmer. Above the Keyboard area is a horizontal scroll bar, which you can click and drag to see information that might otherwise be off-screen.

- **Tab Bar Area**—Located just below the Keyboard area is the Tab Bar area, which displays the key range for the device selected in the Device area, provided that Receive Notes is activated for the device. You can resize a key range by clicking and dragging the boundary handles at either edge of the Tab Bar area (see Figure 5.9). If you click and drag the left boundary handle, you will see the Key Range Lo value change at the bottom of the screen. Similarly, if you click and drag the right boundary handle, you will see the Key Range Hi value change. Note that moving the left boundary handle will move the Key Range Lo value for all devices simultaneously that have the same Key Range Lo value, and moving the right boundary handle will move the Key Range Hi value for all devices simultaneously that have the same Key Range Hi value. To move an entire key range without changing its size, click on the area between the boundary handles and drag the key range to the right or left. Again, this will affect the key range of any devices that share common low or high keys.

- **Key Range Area**—The Key Range area is located in the middle of the Programmer, directly to the right of the Device area (see Figure 5.10). You can move the key ranges in the Key Range area by clicking and dragging them, and you can resize them by clicking on their left and right boundary handles, the same way you can with the Tab Bar area. Key ranges cannot be adjusted unless Receive Notes is active for the selected instrument device. To the right of the Key Range area is a vertical scroll bar, which you can click and drag to see information that might otherwise be off-screen.

■ **Key Range Lo/Hi**—Controls the lowest and highest note that will trigger any selected instrument device in the Combinator (see Figure 5.11). This parameter cannot be adjusted unless Receive Notes is active for the selected instrument device. To adjust the parameter, click on the parameter value and drag your mouse up or down to change the value. Of course, you can also set the key range by clicking the left and right boundary handles in the Key Range area or by clicking and dragging the left and right boundary handles in the Tab Bar area just below the virtual keyboard.

■ **Velocity Range Lo/Hi**—Controls the lowest and highest velocities that will trigger any selected instrument device in the Combinator (see Figure 5.12). As with the key range, the velocity range cannot be adjusted unless Receive Notes is active for the selected instrument device. Key ranges that have a full velocity range (0 to 127) will be represented with a solid horizontal bar in the Key Range area. Key ranges with less than full velocity ranges are represented by a horizontal bar in the Key Range area, which is filled in with diagonal lines (see Figure 5.13).

Figure 5.8

In addition to providing a visual reference for mapping key ranges, the Keyboard area can be used for auditioning sounds by Alt-clicking on the desired keys.

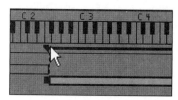

Figure 5.9

You can resize one or more key ranges by clicking and dragging the boundary handles at either edge of the Tab Bar area.

Figure 5.10

Use the Key Range Lo/Hi parameters to set the lowest and highest notes that will trigger the selected device.

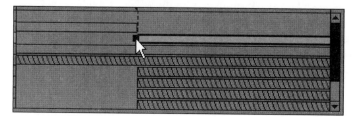

Figure 5.11

Move the key ranges in the Key Range area by clicking and dragging them, or resize them by clicking on their left and right boundary handles.

Figure 5.12
Velocity Range Lo/Hi controls the lowest and highest velocities that will trigger any selected instrument device in the Combinator.

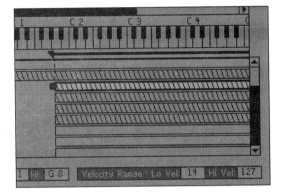

Figure 5.13
Diagonal lines indicate key ranges with less than full velocity ranges.

Modulation Routing Section

The Modulation Routing Section is used to assign any parameters of the device selected in the Device area to any of the virtual Rotary or Button controls on the Combinator's Controller Panel (see Figure 5.14). Unlike the Key Range and Velocity Range settings of the Programmer, the Modulation Routing Section can control non-instrument devices (such as effects), as well as instrument devices like NN-XT or the Subtractor.

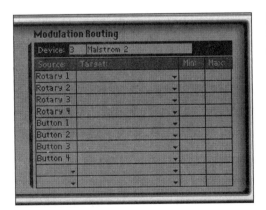

Figure 5.14
The Modulation Routing section of the Combinator's Programmer.

At the top of the Modulation Routing section is the Modulation Routing Device field, which shows the device currently being edited (as chosen in the Device area of the Programmer). Below the Device field are the following columns, from left to right:

■ **Source**—This is where you choose which Rotary knob or Button control you want to use to set the desired parameter on the selected device. Note that while all four Rotary knobs and all four Button controls are listed already, there are two drop-down menus below that allow you to choose any one of the Rotary knobs or Buttons as well. In this way, you could have one Rotary knob or Button control up to three different device parameters (Targets).

■ **Target**—This is where you choose the parameter you want to control with a Rotary knob or Button control. Each Target drop-down menu includes all the parameters for the selected device.

■ **Min/Max**—The Min/Max columns allow you to choose a minimum and maximum value for a virtual control. For example, if a Rotary knob was assigned to control the filter frequency on an NN-19, instead of using the default range of 0 to 127, you could make the far-left value for the Rotary knob be 40 and the far-right value be 60.

The Device Holder

To reveal the Device Holder, click the Show Devices button on the Controller Panel (see Figure 5.15). Now you can see all the devices in the Combi. Under the bottom device is a black space, which is used for dragging and dropping devices into the Combinator. You can also change the order of devices inside the Device Holder by dragging and dropping. If you click in that black space under the bottom device in the Combinator, you will see a bold red horizontal line called the Insertion Line. Whenever the Insertion Line is visible, any device selected from the Create menu will be created inside the Combinator, just under the Insertion Line.

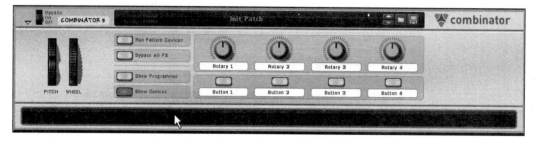

Figure 5.15
Click in the Device Holder to reveal the red Insertion Line so that
the next device you create will be created inside the Combinator.

Using Key Ranges

The following exercise shows how to use key ranges to set up a split keyboard so that you can play one sound with your left hand and another sound with your right hand on the same keyboard.

1. Start with an empty rack and create a Combinator. Of course, it's always nice to start with a 14:2 mixer before the Combinator, just so you don't have to reroute later if this exercise turns into a song for you. Whichever you please.

2. You will usually want a mixer inside your Combis. To create one inside the Combinator, click in the black Device Holder. You should see the red Insertion Line appear at the top. Right-click (Ctrl-click, Mac) on the Combinator and select Line Mixer 6:2 (Micromix).

3. Flip the device rack around (press the Tab key) to see the auto-routing that has been done. The Micromix Master outputs are connected to the From Devices inputs of the Combinator, and the Combinator's Main outputs are connected to the first available stereo input channel on reMix.

4. With the red Insertion Line visible (click in the Device Holder area, if necessary), create two Malströms. Load Saturated Fat into the top Malström, and load Stereo Steps into the bottom Malström. Both patches are in the Malström Patches folder on your CD-ROM.

5. On the Stereo Steps (bottom Malström) rear panel, connect Modulation Input Shift to Mod B output. Set the Mod Shift Trim knob to 3 o'clock (value of 105) and the Shift Target A/B switch to the down (B) position (see Figure 5.16). Now that the Stereo Steps patch is set up properly, flip the rack back around facing front.

6. Click the Show Programmer button on the Controller Panel of the Combinator. If you play your keyboard right now, you will hear both Malströms at the same time on the same note. That is not what we want. Select Malström 1 in the Device area and set the Key Range Hi parameter to E1 by clicking and dragging down directly on the parameter value.

7. Use the horizontal scroll bar at the top of the Keyboard area to scroll all the way to the left. Then click in the Key Range area on the left boundary handle of Malström 2's key range and drag it to the right until the Key Range Hi value reads G8.

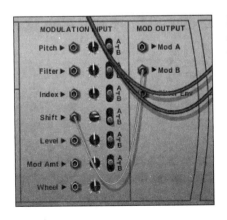

Figure 5.16

On the bottom Malström, connect Modulation Input Shift to Mod B output. Then set the Mod Shift Trim knob to 3 o'clock (value of 105) and the Shift Target A/B switch to the down (B) position.

Now you have a perfect split, and you can play low bass with your left hand triggering the Saturated Fat Patch in Malström 1, while your right hand triggers the Stereo Steps patch loaded into Malström 2. I have saved this patch in the Combinator Patches folder, as well as a short example song using it in the Combinator In Action Folder, both with the name KeyRangeCombi.

Using Velocity Ranges

The following exercise shows how to use velocity ranges to have one synth triggered all the time, while a second synth is only triggered by higher velocities.

1. In an empty rack, create a Combinator. Inside the Combinator, create an instance of Micromix, followed by a Malström and a Subtractor (all inside the Combinator and in that order).

2. Load the Envelope Duet patch into the Malström, and load PhaseArp.zyp into the Subtractor. If you play right now, you will hear both synths at the same time.

3. Click the Show Programmer button on the Combinator.

4. Select Malström 1 in the Device area, then click and drag upward on the Lo Vel parameter until the value is set to 70 (see Figure 5.17).

Now when you play softly, you will only hear the Subtractor PhaseArp patch, but when you play harder, you will also hear the Malström Envelope Duet patch.

Figure 5.17

Click and drag upward on the Lo Vel parameter until the value is set to 70.

Using Modulation Routing

The Modulation Routing section of the Programmer is where you can decide what the Rotary knobs and Button controls on the Combinator Controller Panel will be doing. From a performance standpoint, this is most useful when you can control those Rotary knobs and Button controls with an external MIDI controller.

To assign a function to a Rotary knob or Button control, first highlight the device in the Programmer's Device area, which contains the parameter you would like to control. Then in the Modulation Routing section, select a parameter from the Target drop-down menu located to the right of the Rotary knob or Button control (Source) you are assigning. In this way, Rotary 1 knob, for instance, could control a different parameter for each device in the Device area simultaneously. In fact, it could control three parameters per device. Look at the bottom of the Source column of the Modulation Routing section, and you will notice that there are two Source fields, which are user-definable via a drop-down menu. It should be noted that the Button controls cannot be used to scroll through several values (such as the Filter types or LFO 1 waveforms) The Button controls can only toggle between any two available values. Of course, this can be used for controlling On/Off buttons, among other things.

Let's take the Modulation Routing section for a spin.

1. Start with an empty rack and create a Combinator. Inside the Combinator, create a Subtractor.

2. Load the SawtoothSwell patch from the Subtractor Patches folder on your CD-ROM.

3. Turn the Subtractor's LFO 1 Rate knob up to a value of 80 (a little past 1 o'clock).

4. Click the Show Programmer button on the Combinator.

5. Click on Subtractor 1 in the Device area at the far left of the Programmer. You will see that Subtractor 1 is now displayed at the top of the Modulation Routing Section.

6. Click in the Target column to the right of Rotary 1, and select LFO 1 Amount from the drop-down menu (see Figure 5.18). Now when you move the Rotary 1 knob on the Controller Panel with your mouse, the LFO 1 Amount knob moves as well.

7. To the right of the LFO1 Amount listing in the Target column, click and drag upward in the Min column to set the minimum value to 40. Then click and drag down in the Max column to set the maximum value to 60. Now, even when you move Rotary 1 knob through its entire range of travel, the Subtractor's LFO1 Amount knob will only move between a value of 40 and a value of 60.

8. Click in the Target column to the right of Button 1 and choose LFO1 Wave from the drop-down menu.

9. Leave the Min set for 0 and set the Max for 3. Now you can click on Button 1 on the Combinator's Controller Panel to switch between LFO1's Triangle wave and the Random waveform. As you can see, the values for the waveforms are 0 through 5. The available values for an On/Off button would be 0 and 1.

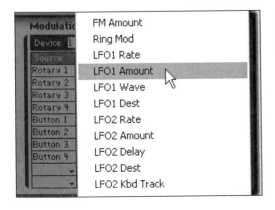

Figure 5.18

Click in the Target column to the right of Rotary 1 and select LFO 1 Amount from the drop-down menu.

Make It Fat

An easy way to fatten up a patch (especially a Subtractor patch) is to create two devices with an identical patch loaded, then pan one device hard left and the other hard right. You can then do something to one or both of the channels to distinguish its audio program content from the other channel's. This could be done with a delay inserted on one of the channels, or it could be done by slightly changing a parameter on one of the two devices. The following example is quite easy and effective because there is random modulation occurring in the Subtractor patch to be used, which results in each device's internal modulation doing different things at different times.

1. Start with an empty rack and create a Combinator. Inside the Combinator, create an instance of Micromix.

2. With the red Insertion Line visible, create two Subtractors. Load StepFilter.zyp (from the Subtractor Patches folder on your CD-ROM) into both Subtractors.

3. Play the patch. If you can listen through headphones, you may have an easier time hearing the change in the stereo image that is about to happen. Move the Pan knob on Micromix Channel 1 all the way to the left, and move the Pan knob on Micromix Channel 2 all the way to the right. Now play the patch and listen to those stereo random steps!

StepFilter.zyp works well in the above exercise because its filter frequency is being modulated with a tempo-synced Random waveform. Since the steps are random, the output from each Subtractor will be different, thus making the left and right audio content different, resulting in a wide stereo image. I have saved a short example song called SteppinCombi located in the Combinator In Action folder, which demonstrates this being used.

Most times, if you load the same patch into two separate synths, and then pan one hard left and the other hard right, you will still need to do something to spread out the stereo image. One easy way to achieve this is to spread the pitch of the two devices a few cents. Turn up the oscillators on the first synth a few cents, and turn down the oscillators on the second synth a few cents. You will get a stereo chorus effect, the speed of which will increase the farther you spread the tuning between the two synths. You may wish to try experimenting in this area with the SawtoothSwell patch (Subtractor Patches folder on the CD-ROM) loaded into the two Subtractors.

Control Voltage, Your Combi, and You

Control Voltage routing may sound rather advanced, but it's actually quite easy, fun, and logical. It's the sort of thing that will come naturally if you play with it long enough. Of course, the great thing about routing CV within a Combinator is that all the connections you make will be saved with the Combinator patch! Here are a couple of little ideas which I hope will whet your appetite for deeper control voltage experimentation.

1. In an empty rack, create a Combinator. Inside the Combinator, create an instance of Micromix, followed by a Subtractor.

2. Load the SineTremelo patch located in the Subtractor Patches folder. Play a few keys to hear what this sounds like.

3. On the Subtractor, turn the LFO 2 Amount knob all the way down. The tremolo effect should have disappeared.

4. Press the Tab key to flip the rack around. Click and drag a cable from the Subtractor's LFO 1 Modulation Output to Channel 1 Pan CV In on Micromix (see Figure 5.19).

5. Flip the rack back around facing front and play your sound. Now you have a nice stereo panning tremolo effect!

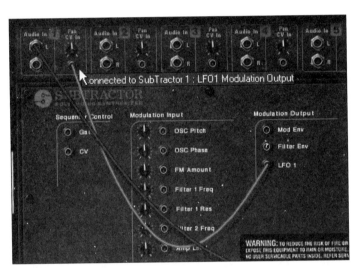

Figure 5.19

Drag a cable from the Subtractor's LFO 1 Modulation Output to Channel 1 Pan CV In on Micromix.

This patch is saved as StereoPanning in the Combinator Patches folder on your CD-ROM. Notice that the LFO 1 CV output is working even though the LFO 1 Amount knob is all the way down. This is because the LFO is always on, and we directly connected Micromix CV In Pan to it. The LFO 1 Amount knob simply controls the amount of LFO signal that will be sent to whatever destination is specified by the LFO 1 Destination control. But what if we were already using both of the Subtractor's LFOs for something else, and we still wanted that stereo panning? Easy! Add another synth but disconnect its audio. Then you have tons of variable control voltage at your disposal!

The next patch is called Redruminator. If you have never thought of this idea before, it should open up a whole new world of Redrum possibilities to you.

1. In an empty rack, create a Combinator. Inside the Combinator, create an instance of reMix. Then create five Malströms, followed by five Subtractors.

2. For the Malströms, load the following five patches from Reason Factory Sound Bank > Malstrom Patches > Percussion: Ambient Blocks, Dinkel, Noise 1, Noise 2, and WavePerc, in that order from top to bottom.

3. For the Subtractors, load the following five patches from Reason Factory Sound Bank > Subtractor Patches > Percussion: Butcher Kik, Chirp, Symbal Song, Syntom, and Zap Drum, in that order from top to bottom.

4. On reMix, spread the pans on Channels 7 through 10 so that they alternate between 3 o'clock and 9 o'clock (left and right).

5. Click in the black Device Holder to reveal the red Insertion Line, then create an instance of Redrum inside the Combinator.

6. Right-click (Ctrl-click, Mac) on Redrum, choose Randomize Pattern, and then click Run.

7. Press the Tab key to flip the rack around. Disconnect Redrum's audio connections. We are not even going to load a kit into Redrum.

8. Click and drag a cable to connect Redrum Channel 1 Gate Out to the top Malström's Seq Control Gate jack (see Figure 5.20). Then connect Redrum Channel 2 Gate Out to the second Malstrom's Seq Control Gate jack, and so on until all five Malströms are receiving CV from Channels 1 through 5 or Redrum.

9. Click and drag cables connecting Redrum Channels 6 through 10 Gate Outs to all five Subtractors' Sequencer Control Gate jacks, in order from top to bottom, as you did with the Malströms.

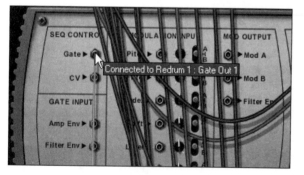

Figure 5.20
Click and drag a cable to connect Redrum Channel 1 Gate Out to the top Malström's Seq Control Gate jack.

You can find a ready-baked Redruminator patch in the Combinator Patches folder on your CD-ROM. By the way, if you don't like the first random pattern you came up with, keep selecting Randomize Pattern until you land on something you can groove to, and modify the pattern as you see fit. Also, you've got tons of percussion sounds in the Reason Factory Sound Bank to choose from for the Malström, Subtractor, NN-XT, and NN-19. And Redruminator is not just for drums! If you are feeling extra experimental, why not load up all those synths with pitched sounds like you would normally play on a keyboard? Who knows what kind of surprises you might come up with using Redrum's Randomize Pattern feature? Remember that all you have to do to tweak the harmonic content is to adjust the pitch of the oscillators on the various synths! Each synth has two oscillators, so you could even trigger two-part harmonies with a single Redrum channel. You could add a few *more* synths and control them with one Redrum channel using the Spider CV Merger and Splitter (in the Create menu). You could adjust the pitch of the oscillators on each synth so that a chord is played each time the Redrum channel triggers the group of synths.

Uncombine/Combine

The two options, Combine and Uncombine, are selectable from both the Edit menu and the context (pop-up) menu. The Combine option allows you to create a Combinator simply by Shift-clicking on all the devices you would like to include in the Combinator and then selecting Combine. To use the Uncombine feature, either select a Combinator in your rack and then open the Edit menu or right-click (Ctrl-click, Mac) on the Combinator to open the context menu, and then select Uncombine. The Combinator will disappear, but the devices it contained will remain with all CV and audio routing still pretty much intact. Of course, you will no longer have any key range or velocity range information, and you will have lost the MIDI routing that is only available in the Combinator.

Combinator Rear Panel

Make sure that Show Devices is enabled. You can then hit the Tab key to flip your rack around and take a look at the back of the Combinator (see Figure 5.21).

Figure 5.21

The rear panel of the Combinator

Audio Connections

■ **Combi Input L/R**—Input for the Combinator, used for effect Combis. In a Mastering Combi, you would likely have the outputs of your main reMix plugged into these inputs.

■ **Combi Output L/R**—Connects with any device outside of the Combinator, usually a mixer, or (in the case of a Mastering Combi) the Reason hardware interface.

- **To Devices L/R**—Connects to the input of any device within the Combi. To Devices L/R is internally routed to Combi Input L/R.

- **From Devices L/R**—Connects to the output of a device (the last in a chain of devices or a mixer) within a Combi. From Devices L/R is internally routed to Combi Output L/R.

CV Connections

Although almost limitless CV routing is possible between the devices within a Combi, the Combinator itself has no CV outputs and has the following minimal complement of CV inputs.

- **Gate In**—Allows the Combinator to receive note on, note off, and velocity information from the Gate CV output of another device, typically a Matrix or a Redrum.

- **CV In**—Allows the Combinator to receive note pitch information from another device, typically from the Note CV output of a Matrix.

- **Modulation Input**—Allows any of the four Combinator Rotary knobs to be modulated by CV.

Combi Backdrops

The last stop on our Combinator tour is not really musical, but you may find it to be a fun feature. The Combinator is the only Reason device for which you can design and load your own skins. Look inside the Template Documents folder located in your Reason folder, and you will see a folder called Combi Backdrops. It contains a very useful explanatory Read Me file, as well as two template Backdrop files. One is a JPEG, and can be loaded as a skin for the Combinator. The second file, Template Backdrop.psd, is a Photoshop document that contains everything you need to start designing your own Combi skins (image editing software not included). If you don't have a program that can read Photoshop files, you can open Template Backdrop.jpg in any bitmap editor and add what you want to it. In either case, save your Backdrop files as JPEGs in the Combi Backdrops folder. Note that any JPEG you use should have a resolution of 754 x 138 pixels. In your Reason song, you can click on Combinator and then choose Select Backdrop from the Edit menu. You will then be able to select a Combi Backdrop from among the JPEGs in your Combi Backdrop folder. I have prepared such a skin for you, which you will find in the Combinator folder on your CD-ROM (see Figure 5.22).

Figure 5.22
Reason allows you to create your own Combi skins. In this case, I have used an alligator skin. Yes, it's the COMBIGATOR!

Make Reason Your Own

I hope that this book has inspired you to dig deeper into Reason and has given you the tools to really take control of the Reason instruments. If you have read all the chapters (including the three appendices on the CD-ROM), and you have gone through all the exercises, then you should have a comfortable grasp not only of the Reason instruments, but also of general synthesis and sampling techniques. You should have a hands-on intuitive understanding of the function of oscillators, filters, envelopes, control voltage, amplitude modulation (AM), frequency modulation (FM) and phase modulation, as well as how to set up velocity ranges and key ranges, and how to come up with original sounding beats using a variety of methods.

The key to creating new and exciting sounds in Reason is experimentation. Taking time to relax and experiment will reinforce what you have already learned, and it will also lead to many happy accidents and new concepts, ideas, and levels of understanding and familiarity. Experiment with all the different things you can do with control voltage. Try adding all sorts of effects inside your Combinator patches. Tweak those filters, adjust those envelopes, discover uncharted territory, and make Reason your own!

Index

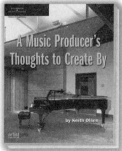

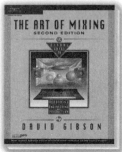

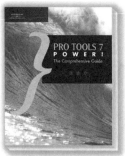

License Agreement/Notice of Limited Warranty

By opening the sealed disc container in this book, you agree to the following terms and conditions. If, upon reading the following license agreement and notice of limited warranty, you cannot agree to the terms and conditions set forth, return the unused book with unopened disc to the place where you purchased it for a refund.

License:

The enclosed software is copyrighted by the copyright holder(s) indicated on the software disc. You are licensed to copy the software onto a single computer for use by a single user and to a backup disc. You may not reproduce, make copies, or distribute copies or rent or lease the software in whole or in part, except with written permission of the copyright holder(s). You may transfer the enclosed disc only together with this license, and only if you destroy all other copies of the software and the transferee agrees to the terms of the license. You may not decompile, reverse assemble, or reverse engineer the software.

Notice of Limited Warranty:

The enclosed disc is warranted by Thomson Course Technology PTR to be free of physical defects in materials and workmanship for a period of sixty (60) days from end user's purchase of the book/disc combination. During the sixty-day term of the limited warranty, Thomson Course Technology PTR will provide a replacement disc upon the return of a defective disc.

Limited Liability:

THE SOLE REMEDY FOR BREACH OF THIS LIMITED WARRANTY SHALL CONSIST ENTIRELY OF REPLACEMENT OF THE DEFECTIVE DISC. IN NO EVENT SHALL THOMSON COURSE TECHNOLOGY PTR OR THE AUTHOR BE LIABLE FOR ANY OTHER DAMAGES, INCLUDING LOSS OR CORRUPTION OF DATA, CHANGES IN THE FUNCTIONAL CHARACTERISTICS OF THE HARDWARE OR OPERATING SYSTEM, DELETERIOUS INTERACTION WITH OTHER SOFTWARE, OR ANY OTHER SPECIAL, INCIDENTAL, OR CONSEQUENTIAL DAMAGES THAT MAY ARISE, EVEN IF THOMSON COURSE TECHNOLOGY PTR AND/OR THE AUTHOR HAS PREVIOUSLY BEEN NOTIFIED THAT THE POSSIBILITY OF SUCH DAMAGES EXISTS.

Disclaimer of Warranties:

THOMSON COURSE TECHNOLOGY PTR AND THE AUTHOR SPECIFICALLY DISCLAIM ANY AND ALL OTHER WARRANTIES, EITHER EXPRESS OR IMPLIED, INCLUDING WARRANTIES OF MERCHANTABILITY, SUITABILITY TO A PARTICULAR TASK OR PURPOSE, OR FREEDOM FROM ERRORS. SOME STATES DO NOT ALLOW FOR EXCLUSION OF IMPLIED WARRANTIES OR LIMITATION OF INCIDENTAL OR CONSEQUENTIAL DAMAGES, SO THESE LIMITATIONS MIGHT NOT APPLY TO YOU.

Other:

This Agreement is governed by the laws of the State of Massachusetts without regard to choice of law principles. The United Convention of Contracts for the International Sale of Goods is specifically disclaimed. This Agreement constitutes the entire agreement between you and Thomson Course Technology PTR regarding use of the software.